Promising Practices to Empower Culturally and Linguistically Diverse Families of Children With Disabilities

A Volume in
Family School Community Partnership Issues

Series Editor:
Diana B. Hiatt-Michael, *Pepperdine University*

Family School Community Partnership Issues

Diana B. Hiatt-Michael, Series Editor

Dedication

To Sherry Buell Alexander,
in loving memory of Diana's younger sister,
who shared decades of life's wonderment with her

Promising Practices to Empower Culturally and Linguistically Diverse Families of Children With Disabilities

edited by

Lusa Lo
The University of Hong Kong

and

Diana B. Hiatt-Michael
Pepperdine University

INFORMATION AGE PUBLISHING, INC.
Charlotte, NC • www.infoagepub.com

Library of Congress Cataloging-in-Publication Data

CIP data for this book can be found on the Library of Congress website http://www.loc.gov/index.html

ISBN: 978-1-62396-631-7 (Paperback)
      978-1-62396-632-4 (Hardcover)
      978-1-62396-633-1 (ebook)

Printed in the United States of America

CONTENTS

FOREWORD

The passage of IDEA 2000 and 2004 marked the commencement of sweeping change at the national level in the field of education of children with disabilities. The history leading to the passage of these pieces of legislation is well documented in Chapters 1 and 2 of *Promising Practices Connecting Schools to Families of Children with Special Needs* (2004). During the years since the passage of these acts, the field of special education has been involved with the implementation of their requirements

The topic of linguistically and cultural diverse (CLD) families was selected because these two segments of special education has received significant attention in the past decade by researchers. The chapters of this year's volume report this research and provide promising practices for the implementation of IDEA for CLD families. The degree of interest in our selected topic was expressed by the number of proposals that we received. After careful review, 30% of the proposals were supported for further development. These chapter proposals were selected based upon their quality but also on the diversity of student ages, practices, and issues facing CLD families within society. The proposals that evolved into the nine chapters for the volume were guided and edited by the co-editors as well as blind-reviewed by scholars in the field.

During the past decade, Latinos have been the largest and fastest growing segment of the American population. Thus, several chapters in this volume deal with Latino programs. However, in 2013, Asian students composed the fastest growing segment. Thus, two chapters describe practices in two

Promising Practices to Empower Culturally and Linguistically Diverse Families of Children With Disabilities, pp. ix–xi
Copyright © 2014 by Information Age Publishing

x   D. B. HIATT-MICHAEL

Chinese areas—Hong Kong and Taiwan—that are of interest to Asian communities in United States.

Mueller anchors the monograph with a description of the roadblocks faced by CLD families. As a guide for promising practices that will remove these roadblocks, she presents a 3-tiered model to assist educational decision makers. This model, if followed, should secure positive parental outcomes for their child's Individual Educational Plan (IEP). The foundation of the model—tier one—is parent education that includes information and resources related to their child's IEP. The next tier is to provide parent support, such as pairing parents and related processes for their child. The final tier is application of a facilitated IEP to assure that the parent voice is accurately heard in the process to develop the IEP. A trained IEP facilitator is added to the IEP meeting to assist the parent to raise questions, receive comprehensive responses, and to make informed decisions. The author's description of Sara's experiences brings the model to life.

Yo, Correa, Anderson, and Swart focus upon social skill instruction as a means to improve self-confidence, motivation, and school social adjustment for Latino families and their children with disabilities. Although this social skill instruction is one aspect of parent and child education, these skills are critical to make informed decisions as noted in Mueller's chapter.

A significant concern to parents and schools is the transition of students with disabilities from high school to higher education, specialized training, and the workforce. CLD families face the added challenges of linguistic and cultural barriers as they attempt to assist their child into the society beyond the public school. Completing the section on practices within schools, Jez presents an approach that trains teachers to assist CLD students and their families to assess and promote knowledge and skills that lead to success beyond high school.

The section on promising practices in the community includes four examples: Evans' grassroots network of Latino families; Miller and Nguyen's program for newcomer immigrant and refugee families; Kalek's encompassing set of parent and child activities/services for young children with developmental disabilities by a dedicated nonprofit; and Aceves and Higareda's programs that promote advocacy skills for CLD families. These chapters were selected because of the powerful impact on CLD families. These chapters contain toolkits that provide ideas and options to work with CLD families. The assessed outcomes of these programs include the understanding of how to educate families so that they may skillfully navigate a foreign school system. Other outcomes encompass the development of the capability to deal with the demands of a CLD disabled child, to support one another in school-related meetings and the IEP, and to promote quality learning environments for CLD families.

The monograph wraps up with two chapters that focus on practices in Asian countries, one in a private school in a dense urban area and the other across communities on an island. Lo, Cheng, and Chan introduce practitioners to the history of education in general and special education in Hong Kong. The chapter continues with a description of the development, implementation, and evaluation of parent support groups in a private school, an example of Mueller's second tier at work in Hong Kong.

Ho, Tang, Detar, and Wang present the background history and describe the particulars related to parent education approaches in Taiwan, examples of Mueller's first tier in practice.

Lusa Lo directed the development of this volume and served as a strong rudder throughout the process. In addition, Lo and I were supported by reviewers from the American Educational Researcher's Special Interest Group—Family-School-Community Partnerships, namely, Martha Allesaht-Snider, Phyllis Hardy, Esther Ho, Barbara Jentleson, Holly Kreider, and Lorna Rivera. Their kind and astute critiques added insight and depth to the quality of every chapter. Lastly, my continuing gratitude to my understanding husband John and to George Johnson, President of IAP, for his support for this series. George's vision and energy propel each volume to fruition and then to readers, the purpose of our endeavor.

Diana B. Hiatt-Michael
Professor Emeritus, Pepperdine University
Series Editor, Family School Community Partnerships,
Information Age Publishing

PART I

PRACTICES IN SCHOOLS

CHAPTER 1

LEARNING TO NAVIGATE THE SPECIAL EDUCATION MAZE

A 3-Tiered Model for CLD Family Empowerment

Tracy Gershwin Mueller

INTRODUCTION

As a parent, Sara had so many questions and felt as if each answered question would lead to 20 more. The idea of moving toward the next step for her children seemed impossible without guidance.

Parents of all children are dedicated to the education of their children (Hiatt-Michael, 2004, 2005). Ongoing research has highlighted the significance of including families throughout a child's educational journey, pointing to academic and behavioral benefits (e.g., Epstein & Dauber, 1991; Esler, Godber, & Christenson, 2008; Spann, Kohler, & Soehsen, 2003). For these reasons, the Individuals with Disabilities Education Act

(IDEA) and its reauthorizations have continued to emphasize the inclusion of parents as pivotal educational team members who should be involved in all educational decisions regarding their child (IDEA, 1997, 2004). The regulations indicate that parents can, including but not limited to, do the following:

1. Access and examine the child's school records, participate in all meetings regarding the child's educational needs, including placement decisions (34C.F.R.§300.501);
2. An independent educational reevaluation, if needed (34C.F.R.§300.502); and
3. Receipt of prior written notice regarding any changes in the child's educational programming (34C.F. R. §300.503).

To ensure that parents are aware of their rights during the special education process, schools must present each parent of a child with a disability with this document annually (34C.F.R.§300.504). In addition, parents are significant members of the school team that develops an individual educational program (IEP) for each child.

ROADBLOCKS FOR CLD FAMILIES

Language

Although parent inclusion is.emphasized in IDEA (2004), research indicates that parents of children with disabilities, particularly culturally and linguistically diverse (CLD) families, experience many obstacles with regard to navigating the special education system (Jung, 2011; Kalyanpur & Harry, 2012). The U.S. special education system is saturated with technical and cultural conventions that can make parental navigation extremely difficult. IDEA is structured so that family involvement requires balancing technical language with advocacy skills within a bureaucratic system among multiple educators for efficient system navigation. For example, the required procedural safeguards that outline parental rights (34 C.F.R.§300.504) are often laden with educational jargon and, to a point, require knowledge of the education system itself in order to understand and apply such rights to a given situation. In an effort to analyze this deterrent further, Fitzgerald and Watkins (2006) conducted a study about the readability of procedural safeguards provided by all 50 states. Findings denoted that only 4%–8% of parent rights were written at or below 7th- to 8th-grade reading level, with 20%–50% of the analyzed documents written at or above a college reading level. Additionally, only a small number of the collected safeguards contained a question-and-answer section. These challenges face all parents but may prevent linguistically diverse parents, who have low English reading level, from understanding the procedural safeguards and exercising their rights.

Culture

Another major roadblock for CLD parent involvement relates to cultural assumptions. The majority culture expects behavior that includes parental questioning and, in some cases, parental challenges of school educator decisions. Yet many minority culture-belief systems and traditions practice an intrinsic reverence for persons of power or influence, thereby promoting passive acceptance regarding a child's educational programming (Cho & Gannotti, 2005; Jung, 2011). These obstacles and relationship dynamics can lead to a perceived lack of family participation by school personnel (Denessen, Bakker, & Gierveld, 2007; Harry, Allen, & McLaughlin, 1995). In the absence of family input during important educational decisions, such as the language of instruction, parent voices may not be included (Mueller, Singer, & Carranza, 2006; Mueller, Singer, & Grace, 2004). Cultural differences possess the potential for conflict that could eventually lead to due process hearings between families and professionals if such families acquire legal advice or counsel (Mueller, Singer, & Draper, 2008). Such passive parent participation and the eventual due process hearings negatively affect the most important party involved—the child.

In short, the U.S. special education system is described as having its own culture (Kalyanpur & Harry, 2012). Countless studies have revealed that parents, who represent the majority culture, typically feel overwhelmed, isolated, perplexed, powerless, and intimidated by the entire process (Childre & Chambers, 2005; Fish, 2006; Lake & Billingsley, 2000; Stoner et al., 2005). Valle (2011) best illustrated the confusion many mothers experience with the special education system by comparing their journey to that of the popular children's story, *Alice in Wonderland*. The author used the metaphor and described the mothers much like Alice going "down the rabbit hole" (Valle, 2011). Therefore, it should be no surprise that families from another culture and/or who are linguistically challenged experience even more frustrations with navigating the system. In an effort to gain a better understanding of this dilemma, researchers have been able to pinpoint some of the more prominent deterrents to CLD parent participation within special education. Some of the most documented obstacles include (a) communication barriers; (b) cross-cultural miscommunications, including nonverbal and verbal communication; (c) technical jargon; (d) definitions of disability; (e) cultural assumptions; (f) attitudes toward interventions;

(g) access to interpreters/translators with a background in special education, and (h) a lack of education/training with regard to special education (Cho & Gannotti, 2005; Jung, 2011; Kalyanpur & Harry, 2012; Lo, 2008, 2009; Tamzarian, Menzies, & Ricci, 2012).

PARENT EMPOWERMENT MODEL

Components of the Model

CLD families are a unique population who require specific strategies for empowerment that can ultimately promote involvement that is culturally respectful and relevant to their membership to the IEP team. Using research in the area of family-professional partnerships, CLD family obstacles and recommended practices, and conflict prevention/alternative dispute resolution strategies, it is recommended that school professionals and local education agencies utilize a 3-tiered empowerment model for CLD families (Figure 1.1). The three major components of this model include (a) family education, (b) family support, and (c) facilitated IEP meetings. All three of these areas promote identifying cultural beliefs, respecting cross-cultural differences, and supporting families by way of adapting practices to meet those values and differences (Kalyanpur & Harry, 2012).

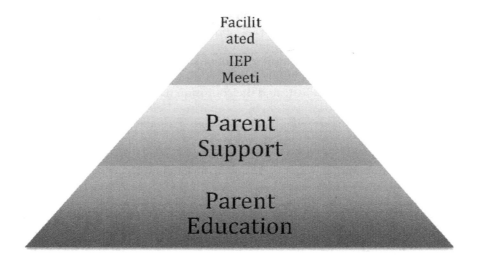

Figure 1.1. CLD Family Empowerment model.

This chapter presents an empowerment model as a means to assist CLD families with navigating the special education system so that they can become active team members and build partnerships with their child's education team. The model is presented as three tiers, with the intent to provide families' universal, targeted, and intensive levels of support, depending on the area of need. However, the model should be viewed as flexible so that at any point all three areas of the model could be used simultaneously, or rather, one family can move throughout all three tiers at different stages. Just as all students are different, families are equally diverse and may require various levels of support throughout their child's education journey.

The following case study will be presented and applied with direct application of each component of this model in an effort to provide contextual application.

Case Study of Sara Martinez

Sara Martinez was a busy mother who worked full time as a librarian and a single parent raising two children who had autism spectrum disorder. Sara's children, Antonio and Cara, were 5-year-old twins who were recently both assessed and qualified for special education services. The school team first approached Sara regarding the twin's educational needs when they entered kindergarten 5 months ago. Prior to entering school, Sara's children were cared for by a neighbor who stayed at home with her three children. Sara and her neighbor spoke both Spanish and some English to the twins. Although Antonio and Cara did not speak much, Sara considered this to be due to hearing dual languages in the home. Sara was never concerned about any delayed language skills prior to entering kindergarten. Although she noticed that the twins tended to socially isolate, family members and friends told her repeatedly not to worry and that it was very typical behavior for twins to socially isolate. Therefore, when the school team approached Sara and discussed the possibility of the twins having autism, she was shocked. Sara was confused, angry, and overwhelmed with all of the information the school team provided her. She did not feel that they asked her many questions. Instead, they overwhelmed her with a great deal of information all at once. Sara spoke limited English and was unable to follow the interpreter, much less apply what was being said. After the initial meeting Sara had with the school team, she walked away feeling deflated and without any idea of where to go next. Her initial confusion set in and began to turn into frustration with the school team. Sara had so many questions and felt as if each answered question would lead to 20 more. The idea of moving toward the next step for her children seemed impossible. This was not something she wanted or felt like she could do alone. But where could she go next? Sara had no idea how to help her children.

Tier I: Parent Education

The foundational area for CLD families of children with disabilities is parent education that is relevant to the parents' culture, the social system, and their child. Mahoney et al. (1999) defined parent education as, "the process of providing parents and other primary caregivers with specific knowledge and child rearing skills with the goal of promoting the development and competence of their children" (p. 131). In the special education field, the IEP is the center of the parent-school partnership. Fish (2006) surveyed 51 parents of children with disabilities regarding their perceptions of the IEP process. Results of this study suggested that there was a need for parents to become more educated about special education and the IEP process in an effort to improve the outcomes of their IEP meetings. Tamzarian et al. (2012) also noted that one of the barriers to CLD family participation in the IEP process is the lack of information and distorted material families receive through the "bureaucratic" IEP process (p. 5).

Because the majority of the information exchanged with families at such meetings is through written paperwork that is loaded with jargon, CLD parents could benefit from opportunities to learn about important topics that relate to their child and family, in their native language, and with respect to their culture. Offering parent education and training topics, such as special education law, terminology and acronyms, IEP, collaboration, disciplinary issues, and transition planning, could enable families to learn and become familiar with the special education process and their rights (Lo, 2008, 2009, 2012a), particularly since the written copy is not often reader friendly (Fitzgerald & Watkins, 2006).

Parent education for CLD families could take many forms, such as traditional lecture style, group meetings with focus topics, videos in native language, and culturally responsive parent-friendly brochures. The intent of parent education is to empower families through information and resources so they can play active roles in their child's educational planning and delivery. Because many districts face budgetary constraints, educators should consider partnering with nearby universities and local community organizations and organizing these workshops. Additionally, each state has at least one Parent Training and Information (PTI) center, which receives federal funding support to assist families of children with disabilities.

Sara Martinez Experiences Parent Education

When educators take the time to educate Sara with the special education process, she will have a better idea about her twins' needs and how she could be prepared for the process. Prior to the IEP meeting, Sara should have the opportunity to attend a district-sponsored parent education class about the IEP process or speak with a school professional (can be the Spanish-speaking parent liaison) who could explain the special education process, Sara's role with the system, and next steps. When Sara is ready, the school will provide her with materials about autism, watch some videos that demonstrate interventions in the home, and acquire materials she can use at home. Sara can gradually increase her knowledge of the special education system and be empowered to advocate for her twins.

Tier II: Family Support

The use of family support within this empowerment model includes pairing families of children with similar disabilities for emotional and informational support. Singer (2002) defined family support as "formal and informal efforts to strengthen families' capacities to facilitate autonomy, inclusion, care, a satisfying quality of life" (p. 148). The practice of connecting CLD families of children with disabilities who may have similar experiences together promises many positive outcomes. The benefits of parent-to-parent support with families who represent the majority culture are well documented (Mueller et al., 2008; Santelli, Turnbull, Marquis, & Lerner, 1997; Turnbull, Turnbull, Erwin, & Soodak, 2006). Some of these benefits include having someone to talk with, being able to access information in a more comfortable setting, and gaining a confidant who understands the system and the experiences that come with it.

In an effort to investigate the use of parent-to-parent support with CLD families, Mueller, Milian, and Lopez, (2009) conducted a qualitative interview study of eight Latina mothers of children with severe disabilities who belonged to a Spanish-speaking parent support group. Interviews with all of these mothers showed this group membership made the mothers feel like a family, allowed them to gain information from one another, and provided them with emotional support. These mothers all shared stories about being there for one another, celebrating successes, holding each other's hands through difficult moments, accessing information, and providing assistance to each other. Some of them even described their small group as "their family."

Sara Martinez Receives Family Support

Looking back at Sara in our case study, the district could provide Sara with another Spanish-speaking parent who is more experienced and has an older child who has autism and has consequently been receiving special education services for a period of time. This experienced parent could meet with Sara and share with her about what special education entails, how her children's needs can be addressed through IDEA, and Sara's parent role within the entire process. The parent could become available to Sara for emotional support as she experiences confusion, frustration, and the sadness that can sometimes take place when a child is identified with a disability. They could talk about autism and what it means for Sara as a parent when she is in her home and community. Later, as Sara begins to acquire more questions, her parent support liaison can answer those for her or point Sara in the right direction, such as parent education opportunities. This level of support could provide Sara with the support that she needs at varying stages.

Tier III: Facilitated IEP Meetings

A power imbalance between families and professionals can easily occur during the IEP meeting, thereby affecting a parent's ability to actively participate (Lake & Billingsley, 2000). One way to address this obstacle and empower families throughout the IEP process is by facilitating IEP meetings using a purposeful parent-friendly structure, commonly referred to as facilitated IEPs. Although a relatively new practice, facilitated IEPs include the use of a neutral person, such as a district administrator from another school, a special education colleague who does not work directly with the student, and a community volunteer, who essentially conducts the meeting by moving the team through the IEP agenda and assuring that there is agreement with each team member before moving through the agenda. The facilitator uses organizational strategies throughout the IEP meeting in an effort to move through the process in a collaborative way, such as preplanning IEP meetings that require contacting parents prior to the IEP meeting about their goals, needs, and concerns for the child. Lo (2012b) also mentions that facilitated IEPs can provide CLD families with a supportive environment that encourages them to be involved in the process. She recommends additional practices during facilitated IEPs, such as arranging a comfortable environment, welcoming parents, and consultation with interpreters prior to the meeting to discuss special education terminology. Other helpful tools include creating and following an IEP agenda, utilizing meeting norms in an effort to ensure that all IEP members are provided with the opportunity to participate, displaying charts/visuals providing information for all to view throughout the meeting, and utilizing a designated "parking lot" space to document issues that are off-topic to the meeting agenda and will be addressed at a later date (Mueller, 2009).

Many states, such as Wisconsin, Pennsylvania, and Ohio, have begun adopting the use of facilitated IEPs through the Department of Education. In 2012, The American Association of School Administrators (AASA) conducted a survey of 200 special education superintendents across the nation and found that 75% of the participants supported the use of facilitated IEPs (Pudelski, 2013). Furthermore, the state of Wisconsin evaluated the use of facilitators between the years 2004 and 2011 and found that 87% of IEP members, such as parents and district members, were satisfied with the facilitative IEP process, and 86% of those respondents would use the process again. Some 86% of the participants reported that, after the use of facilitators, they did not feel pressured to agree with the IEP (Consortium for Appropriate Dispute Resolution in Special Education, 2012). This finding suggests that the power imbalance was removed for these participants during their facilitated IEP meetings. Research in the area of dispute resolution in special education has also identified facilitated IEPs as an effective conflict-resolution strategy between parents and districts (Mueller et al., 2008).

Sara Martinez Attends a Facilitated IEP

Sara, in our case study, could benefit from an IEP facilitator. The facilitator could contact Sara prior to the meeting to explain the process, answer any questions, and ask Sara what she hopes to accomplish during the meeting. The facilitator could also recommend any family education opportunities that might assist Sara with preparation for the meeting. Next, the facilitator and interpreter would meet prior to the meeting, when they would discuss any specific topics or jargon that might come up during the meeting so that they can plan ahead for interpreting technical language. Throughout the process, Sara would be asked open-ended questions, and she would be encouraged to participate while the facilitator maintains a balanced level of team participation. Should any disagreements occur, the facilitator could offer the team strategies to work through their disagreements so that a productive dialogue could take place. In keeping with the parent empowerment model, Sara could also invite her parent-to-parent support member to the meeting. The end result of the facilitated IEP meeting would ideally become a mutually agreed-upon program designed to meet the individual needs of Sara's children.

SUMMARY

The model presented in this chapter can transform CLD families through empowerment and support. First, families can become more familiar with the special education system through parent-education opportunities. New or more in-depth knowledge about a child's academic, behavioral, or social needs can assist CLD families with addressing their child's needs in the home and community. Second, a partnership with other families who have similar backgrounds, concerns, and experiences can empower families to learn more and problem-solve within a trusting support system. Given the daunting nature of the special education system, parent support simply helps CLD families feel that they are not alone. Finally, the last tier offers a more balanced, organized, and simple IEP meeting format. Families become more familiar and empowered to become a part of the IEP team.

This 3-tiered empowerment model can assist families as they move their way throughout the special education system. The layered support encourages CLD families to become active advocates for their child and decreases the opportunities for overwhelming experiences. The navigation of special education is no longer frightening to a culturally and linguistically diverse parent or family. Parents become stronger and more informed about their rights and responsibilities. This level of involvement can ultimately lead to a meaningful outcome for the child and family.

REFERENCES

Childre, A., & Chambers, C. R. (2005). Family perceptions of student centered planning and IEP meetings. *Education and Training in Developmental Disabilities, 40*(3), 217–233.

Cho, S. J., & Gannotti, M. E. (2005). Korean-American mothers' perception of professional support in early intervention and special education programs. *Journal of Policy and Practice in Intellectual Disabilities, 2*(1), 1–9.

Consortium for Appropriate Dispute Resolution in Special Education. (2012). *Wisconsin IEP facilitation trend report.* Retrieved January 10, 2013 from http://www.directionservice.org/cadre/exemplar/artifacts/WI-25%20IEP%20 Facilitation%20Report%202004-08.pdf

Denessen, E., Bakker, J., & Gierveld, M. (2007). Multi-ethnic schools' parental involvement policies and practices. *The School Community Journal, 17*(2), 27–43.

Epstein, J., & Dauber, S. L. (1991). School programs and teacher practices of parent involvement in inner-city elementary and middle schools. *The Elementary School Journal, 91*(3), 289–305.

Esler, A. N., Godber, Y., & Christenson, S. L. (2008). Best practices in supporting school-family partnerships. In A. Thomas & J. Grimes (Eds.), *Best practices in school psychology V* (pp. 917–936). Bethesda, MD: NASP.

Fish, W. W. (2006). Perceptions of parents of students with autism towards the IEP meeting: A case study of one family support group chapter. *Education, 127*(1), 56–68.

Fitzgerald, J. L., & Watkins, M. W. (2006). Parents' rights in special education: The readability of procedural safeguards. *Exceptional Children, 72*(4), 497–510.

Harry, B., Allen, N., & McLaughlin, M. (1995). Communication versus compliance: African American parents' involvement in special education. *Exceptional Children, 61*(4), 364–377.

Hiatt-Michael, D. B. (2004). Connecting schools to families of children with special needs. In D. B. Hiatt-Michael (Ed.), *Promising practices connecting schools to families of children with special needs* (pp. 1–14). Charlotte, NC: Information Age.

Hiatt-Michael, D. B. (2005). Global overview of family-school involvement. In D. B. Hiatt-Michael (Ed.), *Promising practices for family involvement in schooling across the continents* (pp. 1–12). Charlotte, NC: Information Age.

Individuals with Disabilities Education Act. (1997). PL 105-17, 20 USC § 1400 *et seq*

Individuals with Disabilities Education Improvement Act of 2004, PL 108-446, 118 Stat. 2647. (2004). Retrieved from http://www.ed.gov/policy/speced/guid/idea/idea2004.html

Jung, A. W. (2011). Individualized education programs (IEPs) and barriers for parents from culturally and linguistically diverse backgrounds. *Multicultural Education, 19*(3), 21–25.

Kalyanpur, M., & Harry, B. (2012). *Culture in special education: Building reciprocal family-professional relationships.* Baltimore, MD: Paul H. Brookes.

Lake, J. F., & Billingsley, B. S. (2000). An analysis of factors that contribute to parent-school conflict in special education. *Remedial and Special Education, 21*(4), 240–256.

Lo, L. (2008). Chinese families' level of participation and experiences in IEP meetings. *Preventing School Failure, 53*(1), 21–27.

Lo, L. (2009). Collaborating with Chinese families of children with hearing impairments. *Communication Disorders Quarterly, 30*(2), 97–102.

Lo, L. (2012a). Preparing Chinese immigrant parents of children with disabilities to be school partners. In A. Honigsfeld & A. Cohan (Eds.), *Breaking the mold of education for culturally and linguistically diverse students* (pp. 95–102). Lanham, MD: Rowman & Littlefield Education.

Lo, L. (2012b). Demystifying the IEP process for diverse parents of children with disabilities. *Teaching Exceptional Children, 44*(3), 14–20.

Mahoney, G., Kaiser, A., Girolametto, L., MacDonald, J., Robinson, C., Safford, P., & Spiker, D. (1999). Parent education in early intervention: A call for renewed focus. *Topics in Early Childhood Special Education, 19*(3), 131–140.

Mueller, T. G. (2009). Appropriate dispute resolution: A new agenda for special education policy. *Journal of Disability Policy Studies, 20*(1), 4–13.

Mueller, T. G., Milian, M., & Lopez, M. L. (2009). Latina mothers' views of a parent-to-parent support group in the special education system. *Research and Practice for Persons with Severe Disabilities, 34*(3/4), 1–10.

Mueller, T. G., Singer, G. H. S., & Carranza, F. (2006). A national survey of the educational planning and language instruction practices for students with moderate to severe disabilities who are English language learners. *Research and Practice for Persons with Severe Disabilities, 31*(3), 242–254.

Mueller, T. G., Singer, G. H. S., & Draper, L. (2008). Reducing parental dissatisfaction with special education in two school districts: Implementing conflict prevention and alternative dispute resolution. *Journal of Educational and Psychological Consultation, 18*(3), 191–233.

Mueller, T. G., Singer, G. H. S., & Grace, E. J. (2004). The Individuals with Disabilities Education Act and California proposition 227: Implications for English language learners. *Bilingual Research Journal, 28*(2), 231–252.

Pudelski, S. (2013, April). *Rethinking special education due process: AASA IDEA Reauthorization proposals Part 1*. Alexandria, VA: American Association of School Administrators.

Santelli, B., Turnbull, A., Marquis, J., & Lerner, E. (1997). Parent-to-parent programs: A resource for parents and professionals. *Journal of Early Intervention, 21*(1), 73–83.

Singer, G. H. S. (2002). Suggestions for a pragmatic program of research on families and disability. *The Journal of Special Education, 36*, 148–154.

Spann, F. J., Kohler, F. W., & Soehsen, D. (2003). Examining parents' involvement in and perceptions of special education services: An interview with families in a parent support group. *Focus on Autism and Other Developmental Disabilities, 18*, 228–237.

Stoner, J. B., Bock, S. J., Thompson, J. R., Angell, M. E., Heyl, B. S., & Crowley, E. P. (2005). Welcome to our world: Parent perceptions of interactions between parents of young children with ASD and education professionals. *Focus on Autism and Other Developmental Disabilities, 20*(1), 39–51.

Tamzarian, A., Menzies, H. M., & Ricci, L. (2012). Barriers to full participation in the individualized education program for culturally and linguistically diverse parents. *Journal of Special Education Apprenticeship, 1*(2), 1–11.

Turnbull, A., Turnbull, R., Erwin, E., & Soodak, L. (2006). *Families, professionals, and exceptionality: Collaborating for empowerment.* Upper Saddle River, NJ: Prentice-Hall.

Valle, J. W. (2011). Down the rabbit hole: A commentary about research on parents and special education. *Learning Disabilities Quarterly, 34*(3), 183–190. doi:10.1177/0731948711417555

CHAPTER 2

FAMILY INVOLVEMENT IN CULTURALLY RESPONSIVE SOCIAL SKILL INSTRUCTION FOR LATINO STUDENTS WITH DISABILITIES

**Ya-yu Lo, Vivian I. Correa,
Adrienne L. Anderson, and Katherine Swart**

BACKGROUND

Latinos have been the most rapidly growing population of students in American public schools during the past decade, representing a heterogeneous group from diverse countries of origin (e.g., Mexico, Cuba, Puerto Rico, South or Central America). According to the National Center for Education Statistics (NCES) 2012 Condition of Education report (Aud, Fox, & KewalRamani, 2012), Latino students attending public schools increased from 12% (5.1 million students) in 1990 to 23% (12.1 million students) in 2010, compared to a 13% and 2% decrease in White and Black student populations, respectively. (Note that the terms "Latino" and "Hispanic"

Promising Practices to Empower Culturally and Linguistically Diverse Families of Children With Disabilities, pp. 15–32
Copyright © 2014 by Information Age Publishing
All rights of reproduction in any form reserved.

15

are used interchangeably in this chapter.) These Latino students may either be newly immigrants, or as second- or third-generation children (Pew Hispanic Center, 2004), but all come with unique family histories and values that influence their integration into the dominant school cultures (Leidy, Guerra, & Toro, 2012).

Despite diligent efforts to improve educational outcomes of Latino students and to equalize the playing field for culturally and linguistically diverse learners, Latino students experience the highest dropout rate of all minority groups, with large gaps in academic achievement lagging behind their non-Latino peers (Aud et al., 2010; Pew Hispanic Center, 2004). For example, the 2012 NCES Condition of Education report (Aud et al., 2012) indicated that 15.1% of Latinos educated in the United States drop out of school without receiving a high school credential (i.e., either a diploma or an equivalency credential such as a General Educational Development [GED] certificate), almost double that of any other ethnicity (i.e., Black, 8.0%; White, 5.1%; Asian, 4%; Indian, 7.4%).

Further, disproportionality of Latino students in special education presents a concern for parents, educators, and community members (Harry & Klingner, 2006). In states and districts that are heavily populated by Latino students, overrepresentation, especially in the categories of learning disability or speech and language disability, exists (Sullivan, 2011); while in other locations, Latino students are underrepresented in special education (Levinson et al., 2007). The concern in disproportionality not only lies in the overrepresentation that can place Latino students in triple jeopardy with a greater likelihood of (a) being misidentified as having disabilities; (b) being placed in most restrictive settings; and (c) receiving limited access to rigorous academic curriculum (Losen, 2002), but also lies in the underrepresentation that prevents Latino students from receiving appropriate specialized education (Levinson et al., 2007).

In addition to disproportionate representations in special education, Latino students with or without disabilities are at higher risk for social isolation, peer rejection, and overall poor social adjustment in schools (Chang et al., 2007). Latino students often experience higher levels of social, emotional, and economic stressors than their non-Latino counterparts due to harsh living conditions (e.g., poverty, lower parental education, parental absence resulting from overemployment, unsafe neighborhoods, and limited community resources), substandard instructional resources, and discrimination or cultural insensitivity in the classroom (Leidy et al., 2012; Schneider, Martinez, & Owens, 2006). A cultural mismatch may exist between what teachers expect from Latino students and how students behave within formal classrooms. The mismatch may be partly due to differences in values, beliefs, and attitudes between teachers and Latino students (Ford, 2012). Galindo and Fuller (2010) found that teachers from the majority cultural group rated Latino children from economically poor backgrounds lower in social competence than White children; and that there were significant differences among countries of origin, with Puerto Rican and Mexican children having the widest disparities in social competence as compared to Cuban and South American children.

Further, educators may also mischaracterize Latino students as being uninterested, withdrawn, or socially incompetent, possibly due to lack of sociocultural understanding (Cartledge & Kourea, 2008). For instance, Latino students may have friendship networks often exclusive to Spanish-speaking peers due to their strong family unity and bound within the same cultural friendship circle, resulting in being perceived as lack of collaboration with other cultural groups (Lo, Correa, & Anderson, 2013). The "cultural deficit thinking" (i.e., biases in conceptions of race and socioeconomic status of Latino students), combined with inadequate institutional safeguards for supporting teachers in meeting the needs of at-risk Latino students, may have contributed to disproportionality in special education and lower social competence for Latino students (Ahram, Fergus, & Noguera, 2011, p. 2245). If teachers are not culturally responsive to Latino students, this could lead to continued bias, low expectations, and exclusionary practices (Ochoa, 2007). Supporting Latino students with and without disabilities in building social competence in American schools through culturally responsive instruction is indisputably essential.

Culturally responsive social skill instruction is a means to improve self-confidence, motivation, and overall social adjustment of Latino students with and without disabilities within U.S. schools (Cartledge & Kourea, 2008; Gay, 2002). This form of instruction can prompt educators to become culturally aware of biases that can affect lower instructional expectations of Latino students and provide students with skills to appropriately interact with others (Ford & Kea, 2009). Culturally responsive social skill instruction refers to teaching appropriate social behaviors tailored to a specific environment such as school or home while incorporating native culture within the instruction (Robinson-Ervin, Cartledge, & Keyes, 2011). When developing culturally responsive social skill instruction for Latino students, teachers must first become aware of any possible cultural deficit views they may have about the Latino culture and then make a conscious effort to gain knowledge about the origins, traditions, and family life of Latino students. Culturally responsive teachers also use a lens of cultural sensitivity to accurately identify specific social skills that Latino students will require to become socially competent in American schools. The success of culturally responsive social skill instruction for Latino students relies on families' involvement with school, as research suggests a strong correlation between family involvement and improved social achievement (Day-Vines & Terriquez, 2008; Sheldon, 2003; Waterman & Harry, 2008). Latino family involvement in social skill instruction can help teachers (a) understand the impact that culture has on the Latino children's social behaviors, (b) target critical and socially valid skills (e.g., cross-cultural peer relationships) for instruction, (c) integrate meaningful cultural experiences and/or relevant materials (e.g., Mexican literature or folktales), (d) integrate support for language needs (e.g., explaining key vocabulary in Spanish or with pictorial/visual cues to increase comprehension), and (e) promote generalization of the skills in the home and community settings.

In many Latino cultures, the family (*familismo*) is a particularly important concept to understand. *Familismo* means placing the family before one's own personal needs (Leidy et al., 2012). For Latinos, family includes both the nuclear family and the extended family. The U.S. Census Bureau (2011) reported that 78% of Latino households were family households that consist of immediate and extended family members (e.g., grandparents, grandchildren, aunts, uncles, cousins). Latinos have more frequent contacts with extended family members than do White non-Hispanics (Comeau, 2012). The Latino families' interconnectedness may provide a protective factor for children experiencing the stresses of learning a new language and adapting to the U.S.-dominant school culture (Leidy et al., 2012).

Many Latino families socialize their children to value "good comportment and respectful communication (*bien educado, respeto*), cooperation, and caring for peers (*cariño*)" (Galindo & Fuller, 2010, p. 579). Although these values may serve Latino children well in the home, they may not be translated exactly the way they are viewed at home into the formal school culture. Additionally, Latino families may neither be aware of the impact that acculturation to school and second-language acquisition have on the social and emotional development of the Latino children, nor have the time for or understand the importance of structuring home learning activities for their children (Galindo & Fuller, 2010). Cultural differences, language barriers, and social isolation all have been reported as barriers to family engagement in schools and effective home-school communication for Latino students (Al-Hassan & Gardner, 2002; Leidy et al., 2012; Ramirez, 2003). Therefore, teachers must understand the unique challenges faced by Latino families in order to develop culturally sensitive and responsive family-based interventions targeted at developing social competence in Latino children (Dotson-Blake, Foster, & Gressard, 2009).

THREE LEVELS OF FAMILY INVOLVEMENT IN CULTURALLY RESPONSIVE SOCIAL SKILL INSTRUCTION

In this chapter, we discuss three levels of family involvement in implementing culturally responsive social skill instruction with Latino students with and without disabilities: basic level, moderate level, and intensive level. The strategies discussed at each level of family involvement are intended for educators to build culturally responsive family-school collaboration, as well as to engage and empower Latino families in promoting social competence of Latino children with and without disabilities.

Basic Level of Family Support

The basic level of family involvement includes a variety of universal supports and strategies that can be utilized when working with families of Latino children within the context of social skill development. This type of involvement may already exist in many classrooms, with some variations based on teachers' instructional styles and school-family relationship. Recommended approaches at this level include interactions that can be casual or formal, with the use of written and verbal reciprocal communication methods, in addition to meetings with teachers, which involve the sharing of pertinent information about social skill instruction implementation and Latino child's progress in skill demonstration (Waterman & Harry, 2008). Below, we discuss three strategies at the basic level of family involvement, including (a) culturally responsive open communication, (b) parent-teacher conferences, and (c) parent questionnaires, ratings, and/or interviews.

Culturally Responsive Open Communication

Open communication between the home and school is essential for enhancing positive family involvement. To ensure that information is presented in a manner that is both clear and concise, teachers must utilize the preferred language and communication mode of the Latino families when applicable or provide access to professionally trained interpreters to assist in the communication. Teachers may use phone calls to inform parents of their child's positive demonstration of social skills in school as an important part of culturally responsive social skill instruction. This encourages the child's continued use of the social skills and serves as a prompt for the parents to deliver compliments or recognition about their child's skill demonstration. Families may benefit from having teachers provide them with specific examples of what the positive demonstration of social skills looked like (e.g., inviting a peer from a different culture group to join a group) and how they may be involved in recognizing the child's effort and learning outcomes. In addition to the phone calls, ongoing (daily, weekly, and/or monthly) home-school communication logs provide another way to involve Latino families in culturally responsive social skill instruction. The communication logs may be in a traditional format of a notebook or journals, or it may be in electronic format through e-mails, discussion boards, blogs, or teacher's website. As teachers develop and implement culturally responsive social skill instruction programs, they may include the targeted social skills in the home-school communication logs to inform parents about the skills being taught and reinforced at school, as well as their child's progress in learning these skills (Adams, Womack, Shatzer, & Caldarella, 2010).

Teachers must also afford Latino families the opportunities to ask questions or offer comments to facilitate reciprocal communication (Waterman & Harry, 2008). For example, including an area for signature and comments (e.g., ratings of observed social skills at home, skill areas for improvement) on the daily home-school communication notebook is a viable example. If electronic communication methods are used, teachers can designate a specific area on the website or blog where families can make comments about the social skill instruction program. Finally, whenever possible, teachers can make an attempt to engage in brief, positive dialogue with family members upon arrival at school and dismissal. The brief dialogue may involve teachers informing parents about the Latino child's social interactions with others in school, the social skill instruction being provided, and the child's learning progress. The dialogue may also provide a valuable opportunity for teachers to invite families to visit the child's classroom or to suggest ways to further support the Latino child. These strategies can likely allow teachers to build a sense of trust from the Latino families and to strengthen knowledge regarding the Latino families' diverse structures.

Parent-Teacher Conferences

Participating in parent-teacher conferences is a common expectation for all families who have children with and without disabilities. Periodic parent-teacher conferences can allow and encourage healthy communication and relationship building. Parent-teacher conferences can serve as a valuable vehicle for teachers to gain additional knowledge in areas, including (a) the Latino culture from the families' perspective, (b) social behavior expectations at home and in school, (c) social skill success as well as the difficulties the Latino child experiences across settings, (d) possible ways to enhance the child's social skill learning, and (e) ways to integrate cultural responsiveness into the social skill instruction. Promoting generalization of these skills across the home and community settings is also a primary goal of parent-teacher conferences.

When scheduling the teacher-parent conferences, it is essential to attend to the Latino families' schedule and provide flexible conference dates and times to accommodate the families' needs. It is also critical for teachers to acknowledge diversity in the Latino's family structure and be respectful of the Latino culture during the teacher-parent conferences and beyond. By meeting face-to-face, teachers and families can work together to target critical and socially valid skills (e.g., cross-cultural peer relationships) for instruction. Moreover, these conferences can provide teachers with the additional knowledge necessary for integrating meaningful cultural experiences and relevant materials into the classroom. Parent-teacher conferences can be effective ways for Latino families to be involved in increasing the social development of children when they are conducted with the families' best interests in mind to promote a mutual respect (Waterman & Harry, 2008).

Parent Questionnaires, Ratings, and/or Interviews

Parents and family members can be involved in completing questionnaires or social skill rating scales that can help teachers identify essential social skills for instruction with Latino students. These tools can provide pertinent information regarding the observed social skills at home and in the community, as well as the importance of these skills to Latino families and to their children. Additionally, the gathered information from questionnaires and interviews will allow teachers to identify appropriate skills for instruction, taking into consideration Latino family's input.

The Social Skills Improvement System (SSIS; Gresham & Elliott, 2008) is one example that offers multirater forms (i.e., teacher, student, and parent forms) to provide a comprehensive picture of a child's social skills, problem behaviors, and academic competence across school, home, and community settings. The parent form has a Spanish version that will allow Latino parents or caregivers to rate their child's social and academic behaviors. According to Gresham and Elliott (2008), the Spanish version of the parent form has a readability of fifth grade or lower. The translation takes into consideration using terms and expressions familiar to most native speakers of Spanish regardless of the country of origin. Specifically, in the area of social skills, this evidence-based tool focuses on communication, cooperation, assertion, responsibility, empathy, engagement, and self-control (Gresham & Elliott, 2008). For each item, the rater will indicate the importance of each social skill using a 3-point scale (i.e., Not Important, Important, Critical) and the perceived occurrence frequency using a 4-point scale (i.e., Never, Seldom, Often, Almost Always). Completion of the rating will provide teachers with useful information to assess the Latino student's social skill development, which can then be used to identify specific skills for instruction and to evaluate the effects of social skill programs.

Teachers who may not have access to commercial products, such as SSIS, could choose to construct a short questionnaire or conduct a brief interview with Latino families in order to learn more about the Latino culture and to identify culturally responsive materials appropriate for social skill instruction. When interviewing parents, teachers could ask questions, such as What are your child's likes and dislikes? What did you observe as your child's social skill strengths and areas for improvement? What social skills do you feel are important for your child to possess at home, in school, and in the community? Responses from the Latino families can serve as important foundation for developing culturally responsive social skill instruction lesson plans and related instructional materials.

Moderate Level of Family Involvement

The moderate level of family involvement requires an enhanced systems-based approach to coordinate collaboration with families of Latino students with and without disabilities, which helps ensure social skill success above and beyond the universal supports suggested in the basic level of family involvement. Advanced strategies included in this section are to be used in conjunction with the strategies suggested in the basic level of family involvement for optimal outcomes. For the moderate level of family involvement, we will discuss four strategies: (a) offering social skill development workshops for Latino families, (b) providing in-home activities for practicing social skills, (c) providing parent volunteering opportunities, and (d) making home visits.

Social Skill Development Workshops for Latino Families

Offering social skill development workshops for Latino families can provide them tools necessary to promote positive social development and coping skills with their children in relation to school, home, and community expectations (Delgado-Gaitan, 2004). When culturally and linguistically diverse families are offered workshop opportunities, they are more likely to develop basic English-language skills while learning valuable information to help their child succeed (Waterman & Harry, 2008).

In preparing for the social skill development workshops, teachers should consider not only offering support for Spanish-speaking families to effectively communicate with their children and school personnel, but also providing opportunities for Latino families to share and contribute to the school's social skill curriculum. Latino families' participation in the social skill development workshops offers an important avenue to forming supportive, long-lasting social relationships and networks with other families, which have been found to be a strong factor for empowering Latino families (Auerbach, 2009; Durand, 2011). Through the workshops, teachers should encourage the active participation of Latino families to make them feel comfortable and relaxed about who they are while participating in interactive features of the workshops to become more skillful at promoting the social skills of their children at home and in community settings. Social skill development workshop topics that may be helpful to Latino families are (a) social skill expectations in school; (b) importance of social skill development; (c) identifying, teaching, and reinforcing social skills at home; (d) parents' roles in children's social skill development; (e) features of social skill in-home activities; and (f) social skill resources for families. It is imperative to make families feel welcomed and valued during these workshops. Some strategies to consider to ensure that parents workshops are welcoming and successful include (a) asking families for input regarding workshop topics and schedule availability, (b) sending information home in English and Spanish, (c) offering transportation and childcare, and (d) planning meetings that occur outside of school as social events and most importantly viewing families as contributors and collaborators.

In-Home Activities for Practicing Social Skills

Parent participation in child-centered activities at home is a key component for increasing the likelihood that Latino children will demonstrate prosocial behaviors in the classroom (Fantuzzo & McWayne, 2002). The purpose of providing in-home activities to Latino families is to incorporate family members' contributions to social skill development and identify ways in which they feel comfortable supporting their Latino children both at home and in the community. For example, teachers may create an activity to encourage family members and children to discuss how individual words and actions have consequences and how they may affect peer relationships or interactions. Such activities can provide opportunities for Latino family members and children to exercise different perspectives and viewpoints.

Another effective social skill in-home activity is to incorporate role-play scenarios for practicing social skills. Creating scripted narratives that provide opportunities for students and family members to role-play specific social interactions within the home, school, and community can promote skill transfer. For instance, once the skill of initiating a conversation is taught at school, the teacher may develop scripted in-home activities in which the Latino family members are to review the skill steps with their child, ask their child when he or she has to use the skill, role-play multiple situations in which the social skill is required, and provide praise to their child for correct demonstration. In order for these activities to be successful, teachers must provide demonstration and directly teach family members before requiring them to carry out the activities at home. These demonstrations could be provided during a scheduled meeting with a family member or could take place in a social skill development workshop.

Recently, Brophy and Lo (2013) conducted a single-subject research study that examined the effects of a culturally responsive social skill instruction treatment package consisting of researcher-led small group social skill instruction in school and family members' implementation of in-home skill reviews and practice with three high school African American students with mild intellectual disability. Specifically, the authors sent home scripted activities in a workbook for parents/guardians to review and practice three targeted social skills (i.e., responding to teasing, self-control, and standing up for own rights) three times per week with their child. The authors contacted the parents/guardians weekly through a letter sent home with their child and a follow-up phone call to ensure receipt. The scripted lessons explicitly guided the family members to review the skill steps with their child, discuss situations when the skill would be used, and practice role-play situations. All the instructions provided by the parents/guardians were audiotaped so the authors could provide further support to families as appropriate to ensure implementation fidelity. The results of this study showed that the parents/guardians were able to effectively implement the in-home activities with their respective child, and all three students improved their skill knowledge during role-play situations. Anecdotal data also indicated students' skill transfer to naturally occurring aggression-provoking situations (e.g., a student ignored and walked away when being teased by a neighbor after school). In-home activities with a similar structure to the study by Brophy and Lo can be developed for Latino families.

When using in-home activities for Latino families, it is important to make sure the duration and intensity of the intervention is appropriate for the student and to use a well-defined, systematic framework that offers content in the family's native language as well as English (Greenberg, Domitrovich, & Bumbarger, 2000). The family member can further share any feedback or concerns about the delivery of the in-home activities with teachers through communication logs or exchanges.

Parent Volunteering Opportunities in the Classroom

A growing body of research confirms that parents have a profound impact on their children's educational attainment (Epstein & Van Voorhis, 2010). Inviting parents to visit their child's school and classroom is a powerful way to create a welcoming environment for Latino families while promoting academic and social growth (Delgado-Gaitan, 2004). Offering opportunities for Latino families to volunteer within the school environment further allows staff and families to work collaboratively on promoting the social development of Latino students with and without disabilities. Volunteer opportunities can take different forms, including serving on parent advisory committees such as parent-teacher organization (PTO) or parent-teacher association (PTA), becoming a "classroom parent," who may help with celebratory activities or interact with children in the classroom to develop appropriate social interactions, or participating in coaching students in extracurricular activities. Latino families' involvement in these opportunities not only can offer teachers, other parents, and students more educational understanding of the Latino culture, but also can enhance families' active participation in their children's education in schools. Volunteering opportunities within the classroom also allow Latino families to directly observe their children's social interactions with others and allow them to provide prompting or reinforcement as applicable. By making efforts to build these partnerships and to include opportunities for dialogue about topics of common interests, teachers can empower Latino families to be an active social behavior change agent for their children (McCaleb, 1997).

Home Visits

Home visits are effective in easing the school and family relationship, and can lead to greater understanding among teachers, students, and families, particularly those from culturally and linguistically diverse backgrounds (Delgado-Gaitan, 2004). Latino students, especially recent immigrants, often encounter conflicts between their home culture and school culture; whereas the teacher's expectations may be in conflict with the child's home responsibilities and expectations (Sue & Sue, 2008). Although social skill instruction may serve students well in the school environment, those taught skills may be translated differently or misinterpreted in the home environment because of cultural differences (Galindo & Fuller, 2010). For example, Latino families may become perplexed by expected social skills in schools that value assertiveness, independence, and achievement, therefore creating conflicts or confusion for Latino children to conform to both the dominant culture and the home culture. Home visits provide opportunities for families and teachers alike to understand the impact that school and home cultures have on the Latino child's social behaviors and allow for personal contact that will create a healthy partnership. Moreover, home visits may provide teachers an opportunity to establish more intensive family involvement wherein coaching or training of Latino families in social skill instruction delivery can take place. The more visible the contact between Latino families and teachers, the more potential there is for improved cooperation and collaboration in supporting the social needs of Latino children (Miramontes, Nadeau, & Commins, 1997).

Intensive Level of Family Involvement

The intensive level of family involvement in culturally responsive social skill instruction refers to the highest level of involvement from the families and often requires adequate coaching and support from teachers. This level of family involvement requires an increased amount of time invested in directly working with Latino children at home on social skill learning, data collection, and monitoring or evaluation of skill performance.

Teachers may involve Latino families in two ways: (a) training families to deliver computer-assisted social skill instruction, and (b) teaching families to collect data and monitor skill development.

Training Families to Deliver Computer-Assisted Social Skill Instruction

Direct social skill instruction has been found to have moderate to strong effect in improving social behaviors of students with and without disabilities (e.g., Maag, 2006; Miller, Fenty, Scott, & Park, 2011). Culturally responsive social skill instruction has recently received more attention and has shown to result in increased social competence in culturally and linguistically diverse students, including African American students (Lo, Mustian, Brophy, & White, 2011) and Latino students (Lo et al., 2013). When engaging Latino families in the intensive level of involvement, teachers can use a computer-assisted social skill instruction program that provides scripted, interactive lessons to support parents or family members as "tutors" to deliver social skill instruction.

Computer-assisted instruction can be easily structured to provide explicit instruction with embedded audio (e.g., English-Spanish translation in audio outputs) and/or visual (e.g., pictorial representations of key vocabulary) prompts to guide students or tutors through the learning and teaching of specific social skills (Rozalski & Moore, 2004), therefore making it an effective and feasible instructional approach for adaption for families. For example, Lo and colleagues (2013) trained four Mexican-heritage 4th- and 5th-grade male students to serve as peer tutors to deliver 12 culturally responsive computer-assisted, PowerPoint social skill lessons with video models on friendship building (e.g., skills related to importance of friendship, starting a conversation, continuing a conversation, and joining in an activity) to their same-age Latino peers. They found that all eight Latino participants increased the number of positive verbal social interactions with their non-Latino peers during recess. All tutors were able to deliver the instruction with high implementation fidelity with minimum redirection from the researchers after receiving one 30-minute tutor training session. Considering the high level of accuracy in the tutoring behavior of the elementary Latino students in this study, it is very likely that Latino parents and family members can also be effectively trained to deliver computer-assisted social skill instruction to support the social development of their Latino children. Research has shown that Latino families can be trained to effectively support the learning of their Latino children through tutoring using technology (Cooke, Mackiewicz, Wood, & Helf, 2009).

When involving Latino families in computer-assisted programs, teachers can provide the families with training that introduces (a) the role of being a tutor, (b) the structure of the PowerPoint instructional content, (c) steps to navigate through the computer program for instructional delivery, and (d) ways to provide feedback and error correction. Through the use of scripted lessons presented via a PowerPoint format with embedded audio and visual support, teachers can greatly reduce barriers that likely prevent Latino families from tutoring their children. Depending on the availability of technology resources in Latino households, teachers may also need to offer additional support in technology usage or in making the computer-assisted social skill instruction program accessible to Latino families through computers at schools or local resources (e.g., public library). For example, computers available in schools often are equipped with basic Microsoft Office software including PowerPoint. Latino families may be invited to come to school to work with their Latino children after school if their schedule permits. Siblings attending the same school or a nearby school will be wonderful tutors due to the easy access to computers and tutoring locations.

Figure 2.1 presents a selected portion of a social skill lesson that teachers can develop for Latino families to use to tutor their children in learning social skills. Teachers can hyperlink the "speaker" icons on each slide to oral reading of the slide's content in English and Spanish to provide the audio support. The hyperlinked audio prompts allow families to listen to the content being read in both English and Spanish, in addition to reading the written sentences in English.

Teaching Families to Collect Data and Monitor Skill Development

Teaching easy-to-implement methods to collect data for evaluating Latino children's social skill development is another way to empower Latino families. The effects of culturally responsive social skill instruction are best determined through systematic data collection that can provide quantitative data on Latino students' skill performance across multiple settings. To be most effective, school staff and family members should use the same data-collection method that will allow the team to compare data and make decisions about the Latino student's skill transfer across settings. Data presented in a graphic format (e.g., line graph, bar graph) can offer Latino families visual feedback on how well their Latino children have demonstrated the targeted social skills over time. For example, teachers can teach Latino family members simple data-collection methods such as a frequency counting (i.e., tallying the number of a targeted social skill) to document their child's social skill demonstration. The Latino family members can then plot each data point on a user-friendly and structured graphing form that is prepared by the teacher to visually analyze the child's progress. Learning data-collection and evaluation methods will likely enable Latino families to be more objective about how well their Latino

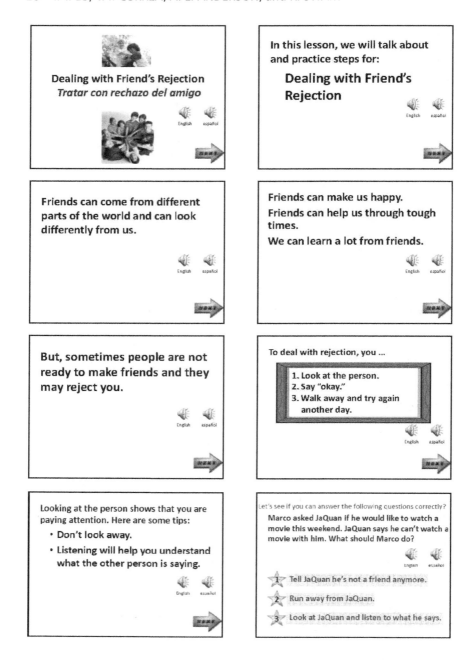

Figure 2.1. Portion of a sample scripted social-skill lesson on "Dealing with Rejection" in PowerPoint format.

children have mastered the social skills and what specific skills are in need of further support. Additionally, the data in graphic format can serve as an important documentation that will increase effective communication and collaboration between teachers and Latino families as the graphed data present a "common language" for both parties.

CONCLUSION

Families are considered the heartbeat or core of schools (Auerbach, 2009). To support Latino students at risk for social isolation and social rejection, family involvement in culturally responsive social skill instruction is essential. Culturally responsive teaching involves creating positive affirming environments in which Latino students can "define themselves and their ethnic identity according to the positive, orderly elements that constitute the basis and aspirations of all groups" without embracing negative cultural stereotypes or accepting subjugated status (Cartledge & Loe, 2001, p. 41). Involvement from Latino families, regardless of the intensity level as described in this chapter, can be a powerful force for educators to maximize Latino students' social learning both within their own subculture and the larger school environment by understanding the Latino culture, teaching critical and culturally relevant social skills, providing language support, and promoting skill maintenance and generalization.

REFERENCES

Adams, M., Womack, S., Shatzer, R., & Caldarella, P. (2010). Parent involvement in school-wide social skills instruction: Perceptions of a home note program. *Education*, *130*(3), 513–528.

Ahram, R., Fergus, E., & Noguera, P. (2011). Addressing racial/ethnic disproportionality in special education: Case studies of suburban school districts. *Teachers College Record*, *113*, 2233–2266.

Al-Hassan, S., & Gardner, R. (2002). Involving immigrant parents of students with disabilities in the educational process. *Teaching Exceptional Children*, *34*(5), 52–58.

Aud, S., Fox, M., & KewalRamani, A. (2010). *Status and trends in the education of racial and ethnic groups* (NCES 2010-015). U.S. Department of Education, National Center for Education Statistics. Washington, DC: U.S. Government Printing Office.

Aud, S., Hussar, W., Johnson, F., Kena, G., Roth, E., Manning, E., ... Zhang, J. (2012). *The condition of education 2012* (NCES 2012-045). U.S. Department of Education, National Center for Education Statistics. Washington, DC. Retrieved May 24, 2013, from http://nces.ed.gov/pubsearch

Auerbach, S. (2009). Walking the walk: Portraits in leadership for family engagement in urban schools. *The School Community Journal, 19*(1), 9–32.

Brophy, A. A., & Lo, Y.-Y. (2013). *Involving parents in culturally responsive social skill instruction for African American high school students with disabilities.* Manuscript in preparation.

Cartledge, G., & Kourea, L. (2008). Culturally responsive classrooms for culturally diverse students with and at risk for disabilities. *Exceptional Children, 74,* 351–371.

Cartledge, G., & Loe, S. A. (2001). Cultural diversity and social skill instruction. *Exceptionality, 9*(1/2), 33–46.

Chang, F., Crawford, G., Early, D., Bryant, D., Howes, C., Burchinal, M., … Pianta, R. (2007). Spanish-speaking children's social and language development in pre-k classrooms. *Early Education and Development, 18,* 243–269. doi:10.1080/10409280701282959

Comeau, J. A. (2012). Race/ethnicity and family contact: Toward a behavioral measure of familialism. *Hispanic Journal of Behavioral Sciences, 34,* 251–268.

Cooke, N. L., Mackiewicz, S. M., Wood, C. L., & Helf, S. (2009). The use of audio prompting to assist mothers with limited English proficiency in tutoring their pre-kindergarten children on English vocabulary. *Education & Treatment of Children, 32,* 213–229.

Day-Vines, N. L., & Terriquez, V. (2008). A strengths-based approach to promoting prosocial behavior among African American and Latino students. *Professional School Counseling, 12,* 170–175.

Delgado-Gaitan, C. (2004). *Involving Latino families in schools: Raising student achievement through home-school partnerships.* Thousand Oaks, CA: Corwin/Sage.

Dotson-Blake, K. P., Foster, V. A., & Gressard, C. F. (2009). Ending the silence of the Mexican immigrant voice in public education: Creating culturally inclusive family-school-community partnerships. *Professional School Counseling, 12,* 230–239.

Durand, T. M. (2011). Latino parental involvement in kindergarten: Findings from the early childhood longitudinal study. *Hispanic Journal of Behavioral Sciences, 33,* 469–489. doi:10.1177/0739986311423077

Epstein, J. L., & Van Voorhis, F. L. (2010). School counselors' roles in developing partnerships with families and communities for student success. *Professional School Counseling, 14*(1), 1–14.

Fantuzzo, J., & McWayne, C. (2002). The relationship between peer-play interactions in the family context and dimensions of school readiness for low-income preschool children. *Journal of Educational Psychology, 94,* 79–87.

Ford, D. (2012). Culturally different students in special education: Looking backward to move forward. *Exceptional Children, 78,* 391–405.

Ford, D. Y., & Kea, C. D. (2009). Creating culturally responsive instruction: For students' sake and teachers' sake. *Focus on Exceptional Children, 41,* 1–18.

Galindo, C., & Fuller, B. (2010). The social competence of Latino kindergartners and growth in mathematical understanding. *Developmental Psychology, 46,* 579–592.

Gay, G. (2002). Preparing for culturally responsive teaching. *Journal of Teacher Education, 53,* 106–116.

Greenberg, M. T., Domitrovich, C., & Bumbarger, B. (2000). *Preventing mental disorders in school-age children: A review of the effectiveness of prevention programs*. University Park: Prevention Research Center for the Promotion of Human Development, Pennsylvania State University. Retrieved from http://prevention.psu.edu/pubs/documents/MentalDisordersfullreport.pdf

Gresham, F. M., & Elliott, S. N. (2008). *Social Skills Improvement System—Rating scales manual*. Minneapolis, MN: Pearson Assessments.

Harry, B., & Klingner, J. (2006). *Why are so many minorities in special education? Understanding race and disability in schools*. New York, NY: Teachers College Press.

Leidy, M., Guerra, N., & Toro, R. (2012). Positive parenting, family cohesion, and child social competence among immigrant Latino families. *Journal of Latina/o Psychology, 1*, 3–13, doi:10.1037/2168-1678.1.S.3

Levinson, B. A. U., Bucher, K., Bucher, K., Harvey, L., Martínez, R., Pérez, B., ... Chung, C.-G. (2007). *Latino language minority students in Indiana: Trends, conditions, and challenges*. Bloomington, IN: Center for Evaluation & Education Policy. Retrieved from http://ceep.indiana.edu/projects/PDF/Latino_Language_Minority_Students_Indiana.pdf

Lo, Y.-Y., Correa, V. I., & Anderson, A. L. (2013). *Culturally responsive social skill instruction for Latino male students*. Manuscript submitted for publication.

Lo, Y.-Y., Mustian, A. L., Brophy, A., & White, R. B. (2011). Peer-mediated social skill instruction for African American males with or at risk for mild disabilities. *Exceptionality, 19*, 191–209. doi:10.1080/09362835.2011.579851

Losen, D. J. (2002). Minority overrepresentation and underservicing in special education. *Principal, 81*(3), 45–46.

Maag, J. W. (2006). Social skills training for students with emotional and behavioral disorders: A review of reviews. *Behavioral Disorders, 32*, 4–17.

McCaleb, S. (1997). *Building communities of learners: A collaboration among teachers, students, families, and community*. Hillsdale, NJ: Lawrence Erlbaum.

Miller, M. A., Fenty, N., Scott, T. M., & Park, K. L. (2011). An examination of social skills instruction in the context of small-group reading. *Remedial and Special Education, 32*, 371–381. doi:10.1177/0741932510362240

Miramontes, O., Nadeau, A., & Commins, N. L. (1997). *Restructuring schools for linguistic diversity: Linking decision making to effective programs*. New York, NY: Teachers College Press.

Ochoa, G. (2007). *Learning from Latino teachers*. San Francisco, CA: Jossey-Bass.

Pew Hispanic Center. (2004). *Fact sheet on Hispanic school achievement: Catching up requires running faster than White youth*. Washington, DC: Pew Hispanic Center. Retrieved from www.pewtrusts.org/news_room_detail.aspx?id=16064

Ramirez, A. Y. F. (2003). Dismay and disappointment: Parental involvement of Latino immigrant parents. *The Urban Review, 35*, 93–110.

Robinson-Ervin, P., Cartledge, G., & Keyes, S. (2011). Culturally responsive social skills instruction for adolescent Black males. *Multicultural Learning and Teaching, 6*(1), article 7. doi:10.2202/2161-2412.1075

Rozalski, M. E., & Moore, L. (2004). Improving students' cooperative social skills with computer-assisted instruction: A summary of a CCBD foundation practitioner support grant. *Beyond Behavior, 14*, 27–31.

Schneider, B., Martinez, S., & Owens, A. (2006). Barriers to educational opportunities for Hispanics in the United States. In M. Tienda & F. Mitchell (Eds.), *Hispanics and the future of America* (pp. 179–221). Washington, DC: National Academies Press.

Sheldon, S. B. (2003). Linking school-family-community partnerships in urban elementary schools to student achievement on state tests. *Urban Review, 35*(2), 149–165.

Sue, D. W., & Sue, D. (2008). *Counseling the culturally diverse: Theory and practice* (5th ed.). Hoboken, NJ: John Wiley & Sons.

Sullivan, A. L. (2011). Disproportionality in special education identification and placement of English language learners. *Exceptional Children, 77*, 317–334.

U.S. Census Bureau. (2011). *Family households, by type, age of own children, age of family members, and age, race and Hispanic origin of householder: 2011*. Retrieved from http://www.census.gov/hhes/families/data/cps2011.html

Waterman, R., & Harry, B. (2008). *Building collaboration between schools and parents of English language learners: Transcending barriers, creating opportunities.* Tempe, AZ: National Center for Culturally Responsive Educational Systems.

CHAPTER 3

POSTSECONDARY TRANSITION PLANNING FOR FAMILIES AND TEACHERS WITH CLD STUDENTS WITH DISABILITIES

Rebekka J. Jez

Students with disabilities often struggle after high school as they enter postsecondary education or the labor force. This is especially true for those who are from culturally and linguistically diverse (CLD) families. These students appear to face additional obstacles during this challenging time in their lives. Many of these obstacles could be mitigated if they had guidance from teachers as well as their families. This apparent lack of teacher guidance may be traced to the lack of knowledge, training, and support special education teachers receive in the area of assisting students through their postsecondary transition (Agran & Hughes, 2008; Benitez, Morningstar, & Frey, 2009). Similarly, parents are often uninformed about resources and supports. Furthermore, they are not asked to provide input during the planning process with their child, and some report they are uncomfortable with communicating with the schools (Kim & Morningstar,

Promising Practices to Empower Culturally and Linguistically Diverse Families of Children With Disabilities, pp. 33–48
Copyright © 2014 by Information Age Publishing

2007; Landmark, Zhang, & Montoya, 2007; Povenmire-Kirk, Lindstrom, & Bullis, 2010).

Research consistently suggests students with disabilities have less post-secondary success than their peers without disabilities (Chambers, Rabren, & Dunn, 2009; Landmark et al., 2007; NLTS2, 2005; Trainor, 2007). With higher dropout rates, lower graduation rates, and less likelihood of attaining success in college and/or training programs, their postsecondary education outlook is dismal (NLTS2, 2005; National Center for Educational Statistics, 2009; Wagner, Newman, Cameto, Levine, & Garza, 2006), which can lead to future problems in the community, such as poverty, unemployment, homelessness, and drugs (NLTS2, 2006; National Organization on Disability, 2004; U.S. Department of Labor, 2008). In 2013, the national unemployment rate was 8% (Bureau of Labor Statistics, 2012). For persons with disabilities, the rate of unemployment was 15%, with African Americans at 24 %, Hispanics at 20%, Whites at 14%, and Asians at 11%. These data indicated that persons with a disability and/or from a racially diverse group are more likely to have a higher risk of being unemployed.

OBSTACLES IN POSTSECONDARY TRANSITION

In order to address education, employment, and independent living skills prior to leaving high school, teachers must work collaboratively with families of their students with disabilities. However, when working with CLD families, previous studies indicated that teachers might not have addressed barriers these families might have faced, such as language issues, concerns about documentation and citizenship, and limited school and community resources (Landmark et al., 2007; Povenmire-Kirk et al., 2010; Trainor, 2007). This may be due to teachers' lack of information and hesitancy to address these sensitive topics.

Previous research has examined the transition planning process for students with disabilities and found that teachers played an important role in facilitating the process and making families feel welcome. Landmark and her colleagues (2007) interviewed 19 CLD parents about their experience with transition planning for their child. The parents' reports on their experience were filled with concerns and frustration. They described frustration with special education jargon, lacking knowledge about their child's legal rights or the expectation for their involvement in the process, and a general lack of "parent-friendly" relationships with the educators at the school. In addition, parents indicated that they had difficulty getting time off from their employers for these meetings at the school. Finally, they shared concerns about having a different value system from the prevalent school pressure to continue into institutions of higher education. Some parents were less tolerant of the value that students should focus on their individual career paths and believed that student's expectations should be on the value as a contributing member of the family unit. This value often took precedence over prevailing educational policies that promote students to advance to institutions of higher education.

In another study, Povenmire-Kirk et al. (2010) used interviews and focus groups with students, families, and school officials to learn more about the issues experienced by CLD students and families. They found that there were three main barriers that these families and students encountered. First, families reported language being a barrier when speaking English and understanding the special education and transition jargon used during the transition process. Second, some parents and students did not have citizenship or documentation, and they were worried about sharing this information with the school officials. Third, there was a concern about teachers' lack of culturally responsive practices when working with CLD youth and families. Many teachers were unknowingly culturally insensitive to the needs and desires of the CLD families.

The above studies clearly suggest that there is an urgent need for teachers to increase the explicit instruction concerning self-determination skills, complete useful assessments and planning for students, and involve all stakeholders. More professional developments for teachers are necessary. This chapter provides information regarding a training program, the Culturally Responsive Summary of Performance (CRSOP), which is based upon a model of six identified self-report skills, and its impact on teachers when assisting CLD students with disabilities and families during the transition planning process from high school to adult life.

CULTURALLY RESPONSIVE SUMMARY OF PERFORMANCE TRAINING PROGRAM

Development of the Program

The CRSOP training program is based on a model that combines the six culturally responsive elements with the six identified self-determination skills to assess if the student had addressed self-determination and culturally responsive practices in their presentation. The self-determination skills that are used in the CRSOP training were adapted from Field, Martin, Miller, Ward, and Wehmeyer's (1998) list of necessary self-determination skills. The skills include self-awareness, self-advocacy, choice and decision making, self-regulation, problem solving, and goal setting and attainment. These six skills complemented Geneva Gay's (2000) characteristics of cultural responsiveness: validating, emancipatory, comprehensive, empowering, multidimensional, and transformative. Table 3.1 compares two scholars' terms used in their models and the self-determination skills applied in this study. The self-determination skills and the culturally responsive practices support each other and provide a description of how the students were able to address culturally responsive self-determination skills while implementing their CRSOP (Chamberlain, 2005; Field et al., 1998; Gay, 2000; Jez, 2011; Wehmeyer, Agran, & Hughes, 1998).

Table 3.2.   A Comparison of Self-Determination Skills According to Field et al. (1998), Gay's (2000) Culturally Responsive Practices, and Jez's Description of Culturally Responsive Self-Determination Skills

Self-Determination Skill by Field et al.	Gay's Culturally Responsive Practice	Description of Culturally Responsive Self-Determination Skills According to Jez
Self-Awareness	Validating	Able to describe the culture(s) he/she identifies with. Student knows his/her disability and helpful accommodations/modification.
Self-Advocacy	Emancipatory	Communicates strengths, needs, interests, preferences, and knows access rights (ADA). Can express this in an appropriate manner (code-switching).
Choice and Decision Making	Comprehensive	Student knows self, value self, gathers information, predicts consequences, plans, acts, and evaluates by weighing pros and cons of multiple factors.
Self-regulation	Empowering	Students show self-management, organization, and self-reflection skills. The student feels confident about his/her skills and ability to meet goals.
Problem solving	Multidimensional	Ability to address issues in a multitude of settings, with various people, and come up with viable solutions.
Goal Setting and Attainment	Transformative	The knowledge, skills, and values to develop long-term and short-term goals that reflect and respect culture: social, racial, linguistic, political, educational (disability), and economic

The CRSOP training program included a 2-hour training session and six weeks of support by the trainer. The complete training presentation included the following four parts:

1. A review of the legal requirements around postsecondary transition;
2. A review of the CRSOP document;
3. Information regarding culturally responsive transition; and
4. Implementation of the CRSOP.

Description of the Training Program

History of Special Education

The legal requirements around supporting youth with special needs have changed since the federal government began addressing marginalized person's needs. The Civil Rights Act of 1964 (PL 88-352) was the first major piece of legislation to address rights and support regardless of an "individual's race, color, religion, sex, or national origin." This laid the foundation for special education services, however, postsecondary transition requirements did not appear until the mid-1980s when Madeline Will put forth the plan to bridge the school to adulthood experience. Currently, teachers are mandated to provide each student who is exiting high school due to graduation or aging out with a Summary of Performance (SOP) (IDEA, 2004). The SOP is a document that includes information on the student's background, reports the results of assessments used in the transition planning, reviews a summary of academic and functional performance levels, and identifies goals and recommendations on meeting postsecondary goals.

Program Components

The second part of the training targets each component of the recommended SOP template and the intentions of the CRSOP program. Participants will learn how to create a document that could support youth with disabilities in qualifying for the Americans with Disabilities Act (ADA). By quickly reviewing the sections of the SOP and showing them where to locate the information in the district's IEP, the teachers can realize what areas of the IEP needed to be improved prior to the student's exit from high school.

Next, the teachers are introduced to self-determination skills and provided minilessons for explicitly teaching the skills to their students (Martin, 2002; Test et al., 2004; Wehmeyer, Field, Doren, Jones, & Mason, 2004). Self-determination skills included self-advocacy, problem solving, decision-making, goal setting and attainment, self-regulation, self-awareness, and self-efficacy (Wehmeyer et al., 1998; Wood, Karvonen, Test, Browder, & Algozzine, 2004).

Implementing the Training

The third part of the training explains how to implement a culturally responsive transition with CLD students and families. According to previous research, three challenges that educators identify having during transition planning and implementation include lack of time, resources, and student and family support (Benitez et al., 2009; Wandry et al., 2008). To address issues of time, a timeline for implementing each activity and opportunities for the trainer's additional support are given to the teachers in efforts to organize and structure the time expended by staff during the CRSOP process. This part of the training includes district-specific resources for support, such as how to complete the IEP using the online IEP database and how to read and report on the results of the psycho-educational assessments used in the most current triennial testing. The training also includes information on how to administer and report on additional formal and informal assessments concerning postsecondary employment, education, and independent living. All of the resources and materials are provided to the teachers along with helpful recommendations for increasing student and family support.

One of the most important aspects of effective CRSOP transition planning is using various formal and informal assessments to understand who the student is and what is needed to reach their postsecondary goals (Field & Hoffman, 2007; Jez, 2011). It is most helpful when students themselves complete and understand the results of academic, behavioral/emotional, career, and personal assessments. Additionally, it is useful to gather input from their teachers, family members, and outside support people such as case managers, counselors, mentors, employers, and such. The more information gathered, the more comprehensive the planning. All of this can be very daunting and time-consuming for teachers and students to find time to complete during the school year (Jez, 2011).

There is a need for students to become familiarized with their IEP and psycho-educational assessment information. For example, if a student has an auditory processing deficit, what does that mean? What are helpful accommodations and modifications that can aid him/her in learning? What accommodations and modifications are not helpful? What are the students' processing strengths and weaknesses? When a student and his/her family are comfortable with this information, the likelihood of the student's ability to self-advocate increases. In addition to finding out about their academic and processing abilities, examining student's emotional and behavioral issues from the perspective of the student, teacher, and family can aid in making an effective plan for their future mental health. One assessment that has been used is the Behavioral-Emotional Rating Scale II (BERS-II), a survey and open-ended questionnaire. Parents felt more involved after completing the BERS-II (Jez, 2011).

The CRSOP recommends students complete assessments to help determine their career interests, skills, and values. There are many free online options with inventories that connect results with occupational and educational information and aid in completing their career assessments. By completing the inventories, students increase their knowledge of different career paths and/or may familiarize themselves with additional occupational pathways. They may also find that a career they had previously thought interesting is the right path for them at this time. In addition, the results provide descriptive words they can add to their self-determination PowerPoint presentation, résumé, and cover letter. This vocabulary is important in our technological age in which online applications and search engines identify keywords when searching for potential employees.

Stages to Complete CRSOP

The fourth part of the training is to present the recommended three stages necessary to complete a CRSOP. First, teachers need to properly assess the student (including assessments from the student, teachers, and families). Student assessments include the online and class assessments on their postsecondary transition plan and self-knowledge. The assessments from teachers provide the student with functional academic levels (current levels, strengths, and challenges with reading, writing, and mathematics), functional performance levels (processing, emotional, cognitive, health), and appropriate accommodations and modifications. Family assessments include the Family Input document, which asks the family about their child's strengths, concerns, postsecondary transition plan, and any existing supports the child receives. Often families and youth have a different perspective on the child's transition plan, and this document can help both parties understand each other. The next step is to gather necessary transition documents such as a résumé, cover letter and applications to other agencies, postsecondary education or training institutions, and financial agencies. Finally, the completion stage of working with the students in completing their Student Self-Determination PowerPoint and SOP documents, which describe their plans for adulthood.

The Student Self-Determination PowerPoint template has about 14 slides. Each slide includes a topic, and there are directions for completing the slide in the notes section. Many slides use the results from the assessments, IEPs, web research students have completed, and support materials provided. A description of each slide is found in Table 3.2 with specific issues students encountered during the study.

At the end of the CRSOP process, the transition team (student, family, teacher, and possibly outside agency representative) attend the CRSOP meeting. The students present their self-determination PowerPoint and SOP document. The team will provide comments and ask questions. Finally, each member will be given a copy of the necessary transition documents, self-determination PowerPoint, SOP, current IEP, and most recent psycho-educational testing results and report.

**Table 3.2.   Student Self-Determination PowerPoint
Presentation Template Slide Topics, Description of Student
Activity, and Teachers' Perception of Students**

Slide Topic	Description of Student Activity	Teachers' Perceptions of Students
Title	The student is asked to create an interesting title that demonstrates that they will be successful after graduation. They also need to write their full name and the current school year.	Many students did not want to write their "government name," however, for this assignment, the name used on their social security card was preferred.
Self-Awareness	Students need to list at least three strengths, interests, preferences, and needs. They are asked to use the results of their career assessments, IEP, and the psycho-educational report to complete this slide.	Most of the students either gave up or rushed through their assessments, however, when they saw how the results were reflected in their PowerPoint, they were willing to retake the assessment to access the correct information.
Self-Awareness	Students are asked to identify their culture (ethnic background, economic background, how their family views education, jobs, and living arrangements), language(s) (how proficient are they in speaking and writing), and disability (describe the label and what it mean for the student).	Most of the students believed culture meant race, however, once they read the slide, a conversation about their families' views began. For many, they were the first to graduate and plan to go to college. Identifying the language gave the bilingual students a feeling of empowerment. It should also be noted none of the students were able to explain their disability prior to this training. While working on this slide, Angel said, "Oh, is that what auditory processing means?"

(Table continues on next page)

Table 3.2.   (Continued)

Slide Topic	Description of Student Activity	Teachers' Perceptions of Students
Postsecondary Transition Goals	Students need to state their employment, education/training, and independent living goals.	Because of the IDEA requirement of identifying transition goals in the ITP portions of the IEP, students had a general idea of what they wanted to do after high school, however, after completing the assessments, many students changed their response. Mr. Diaz reported Hector's change: "At first he wanted to work for Comcast, but after finishing the assessments, he decided he wanted to be a chef."
Americans with Disabilities Act	Students are asked to research how to access ADA services and make a list of potential accommodations and modifications that may help them in school or at the workplace.	In order to seamlessly continue to receive services after high school, students need to (a) register with the ADA office at their place of employment or school/training program, (b) bring in proof of their disability (an ADA representative can request additional testing that may need to be paid for by the youth), and (c) identify possible and plausible accommodations and modifications that work with the establishment. In the study, none of the teachers, students, or families completed this portion. Since that time, additional information and supports were created for training teachers about ADA services.

(Table continues on next page)

Table 3.2.   (Continued)

Slide Topic	Description of Student Activity	Teachers' Perceptions of Students
Academic Abilities	Students use the results from the district academic achievement tests and teacher assessments to identify their current academic levels and areas of need in reading, writing, and mathematics.	Students needed to identify their academic levels and what they meant. For example, Jose said, "I am at the junior high level for writing; I need help knowing where to put the punctuation."
Resiliency	Students identify the stressful experiences they may encounter as adults and how they will deal with stress and meet their responsibilities even though tough situations may arise.	Kevin, who grew up in an abusive family, foster care, and was currently living at a men's shelter, wrote, "Things that stress me out are having too much to do at one time and having no control over what's happening around me."
Helpful Accommodations and Modifications	Students identify the accommodations and modifications reported in the IEP and in their experience that have helped them be more successful academically and socially.	Angel listed accommodations and modifications that are helpful like "repeating instructions, extra time, a calculator, and working in small groups."
Self-Efficacy	Self-efficacy means believing one can accomplish the desired goals in life. Students are asked to write a sentence including specific reasons he/she will be successful.	Abel wrote, "I know I will be successful because I know where I'm going and I know how to get there. I just need a little help from friends and family sometimes."

(Table continues on next page)

Table 3.2.   (Continued)

Slide Topic	Description of Student Activity	Teachers' Perceptions of Students
Overcoming Adversity	Students are asked to explain how they will deal with being treated negatively due to their disability, racism, sexism, and economic issues.	Jose said, he would overcome obstacles by "seeking out help" and "work hard at my job, be on time, dress formally, speak maturely, and be well connected." Many students referred to code-switching on this slide. Angel said he had encountered racism, but his teachers had never talked to him about how to deal with the issue of racism.
Staying Connected	People who stay connected to their community (church, family, neighborhood, friends, etc.) are able to overcome obstacles and become more successful because they have a support system to turn to when life gets hard. Students are asked to identify how he/she will stay connected to their community after high school.	Hector says he will stay connected to the community by having a part-time job, playing sports, and spending time with his family. Other students mentioned church or community centers.
Employment Goal	Successful people make long-term and short-term goals. Students are asked to write a long-term career goal (dream job) and then at least two short-term employment goals (jobs that will help them build their résumé and make some money while they are getting additional training).	Abel's employment goal was to work in an auto body shop. His short-term goals included creating a résumé and cover letter, applying for jobs in auto body shops, and applying for the auto body program at the local college.

(Table continues on next page)

Table 3.2.   (Continued)

Slide Topic	Description of Student Activity	Teachers' Perceptions of Students
Education Goal	Students are asked to write a long-term education/training goal (preferences for college or training) and then at least two short-term education goals (things needed to do to attain the goal).	Kevin, the student in foster care, wrote that he would "apply for the construction programs, take the placement tests, and apply for Free Application for Federal Student Aid (FAFSA) and Chafee Grant for foster youth.
Independent Living Goal	Students were asked to write a long-term independent living goal (where they would like to live and with whom) and then at least three short-term independent living goals. For example, their budget plan, banking goals, driver's license, medical insurance, etc.	Most of the students wrote about getting a driver's license, a bank account, learning to cook, budget, and how to find roommates.

EFFECTIVENESS OF THE CULTURALLY RESPONSIVE SUMMARY OF PERFORMANCE

Evaluation Study

Five high school teachers in a large urban district and seven students with various disabilities and culturally diverse backgrounds participated in the evaluation of the Culturally Responsive Summary of Performance (CRSOP) training program. The teacher participants included two White Americans, two Latino Americans, and one Middle Eastern American teacher. The six student participants were all identified as being marginalized CLD students with disabilities. All of the students were from a culturally diverse ethnicity, five students spoke an additional language at home, six received free or reduced-price lunch, and four lived with their mother, two with extended family, and one student was homeless.

To evaluate the effectiveness of the CRSOP training and support program, teachers were surveyed and interviewed about postsecondary transition and culturally responsive practices before and after the CRSOP training and support program. The survey assessed the teacher's perspectives on training and their confidence in working with students on transition, self-determination, and culturally responsive practices. The initial interview asked open-ended questions about the teacher's educational history, pedagogical practices, and information about the student who decided to implement the CRSOP with during the process. The follow-up interview allowed teachers to review their initial interview responses and evaluate of the CRSOP program. In addition, students were also asked to complete a survey about what their teachers were doing to support their transition planning.

Findings

Many benefits were found for teachers, students, and families. Teachers reported increased knowledge of legal requirements, resources, and methods of best practice. Specifically, after the training, teacher participants reported an increase in the number of transition components they implemented and began to explicitly teach self-determination skills and culturally responsive methods, such as code-switching and discussing how to deal with common obstacles, with their students and families. One teacher said,

> I didn't know how much I didn't know before this training. This is so important for special educators, their students, and the families. I forgot I had to hook them up with other agencies; I didn't even know what those agencies were or which kids were able to access help from them.

The students who participated in the study reported very few self-determination skills in the survey before the CRSOP process. After completing the CRSOP process, all of them demonstrated an increase in self-determination skills and attending to culturally responsive issues as adults. Another teacher and his student had the following exchange: "You said you felt like you got to know yourself better didn't you?" The student replied, "It is important for me so I don't get lost ... I believe good things are in my future."

Besides teachers and students, families also benefitted from the CRSOP process by improving the home-to-school relationships though active participation in the transition process with the school and their child. Prior to the CRSOP process, the teachers reported they did not always involve families, have translators available during meetings, and/or translate documents into the home language; whereas after the completing the process, all of the educators worked at assessing the students differently, working more closely with parents, and making their efforts in the relationship more convenient for the families. Although the families and students' involvement in the transition process was limited before CRSOP implementation, all of the teachers were dedicated to increasing this in the future. This is especially important because most of the students reported their families were very concerned with their transition to adulthood responsibilities.

CONCLUSIONS

The CRSOP training program clearly suggests that when teachers receive training on how to facilitate the transition planning process in a culturally sensitive manner, all stakeholders benefit from the process. Table 3.2 includes a list of action items families can do to increase their participation in the process. By completing assessments, providing input, finding out about their child's legal rights and responsibilities, and showing up for meetings, parents can increase the success of their child. After high school, the teacher and school will not be involved and the major support must come from the families. Having copies of important documents; being knowledgeable about strengths, needs, and helpful services; and supporting the youth's transition planning is essential in providing a foundation to help support a positive outlook for CLD students with disabilities.

There are several ways administrators can ensure that similar training program is accessible to teachers. First, teacher training programs in colleges and universities should emphasize the knowledge about postsecondary transition and culturally responsive pedagogy that students are expected to demonstrate prior to high school graduation. Second, at the district level, administration needs to provide consistent and effective training and support to teachers beginning in middle school. This could be in assessments, personnel for supporting the transition process, and opportunities for learning about educational and career options. Finally, students and families need to be exposed, educated, and empowered in the postsecondary transition process. CLD students and families need to be given a voice, and educators need to learn how to recognize and listen to the diverse experiences, strengths, and needs of each individual to increase the postsecondary achievements of the students in their classes.

REFERENCES

Agran, M., & Hughes, C. (2008). Students' opinions regarding their individualized education program involvement. *Career Development for Exceptional Individuals, 3*(2), 69–76.

Benitez, D. T., Morningstar, M. E., & Frey, B. B. (2009). A multistate survey of special education teachers' perceptions of their transition competencies. *Career Development for Exceptional Individuals, 32*(6), 6–16.

Bureau of Labor Statistics. (2009). [Home page]. Retrieved from http://www.bls.gov/

Chambers, D., Rabren, K., & Dunn, C. (2009). Transition from high school to adult life: A comparison of students with and without disabilities. *Journal of Career Development for Exceptional Individuals, 32*(1), 42–52.

Chamberlain, S. P. (2005). Recognizing and responding to cultural difference in the education of culturally and linguistically diverse learners. *Interven School and Clinic, 40*(4), 195–211.

Field, S., & Hoffman, A. (2007). Self-determination in secondary transition assessment. *Assessment for Effective Intervention, 32*(3), 181–190.

Field, S., Martin, J. E., Miller, R., Ward, M., & Wehmeyer, M. (1998). *A practical guide for teaching self-determination.* Reston, VA: Council for Exceptional Children.

Gay, G. (2000). *Culturally responsive teaching: Theory, research, & practice.* New York, NY: Teachers College Press.

Individuals with Disabilities Education Improvement Act of 2004, PL 108-446, 118 Stat. 2647. (2004). Retrieved from http://www.ed.gov/policy/speced/guid/idea/idea2004.html

Jez, R. J. (2011). *Empowering equity in postsecondary transition for marginalized culturally and linguistically diverse students with disabilities by implementing a culturally responsive summery of performance teacher training and support program* (Unpublished doctoral dissertation). University of San Francisco, San Francisco, California.

Kim, K., & Morningstar, E. M. (2007). Enhancing secondary special education teachers' knowledge and competencies in working with culturally and linguistically diverse families through online training. *Career Development for Exceptional Individuals, 30*(2), 116–128.

Landmark, L., Zhang, D. D., & Montoya, L. (2007). Culturally diverse parents' experiences in their children's transition: Knowledge and involvement. *Career Development for Exceptional Individuals, 30*(2), 68–79.

Martin, J. (2002). The transition of students with disabilities from high school to postsecondary education. In C. A. Kochhar-Bryant & D. S. Bassett (Eds.), *Aligning transition and standards-based education: Issues and strategies* (pp. 167–186). Arlington, VA: Council for Exceptional Children.

National Center for Educational Statistics. (2009). *Fast facts.* Retrieved from http://nces.ed.gov/FastFacts/

National Longitudinal Transition Study 2 (NLTS2). (2005). *Facts from NLTS2: High school completion by youth with disabilities.* Retrieved from www.nlts2.org/fact_sheets/nlts2_fact_sheet_2005_11.pdf

National Organization on Disability. (2004). *Harris survey of Americans with disabilities.* Retrieved from http://www.nod.org/research_publications/nod_harris_survey/

Povenmire-Kirk, T. C., Lindstrom, L., & Bullis, M. (2010). De escuela a la vida adulta/from school to adult life: Transition needs for Latino youth with disabilities and their families. *Career Development for Exceptional Individuals, 33*(1), 41–51.

48   R. J. JEZ

Test, D., Mason, C., Hughes, C., Konrad, M., Neale, M., & Wood, W. (2004). Student involvement in individual education program meetings. *Exceptional Children, 70*(4), 391–412.

Trainor, A. A. (2007). Person-centered planning in two culturally distinct communities: Responding to divergent needs and preferences. *Career Development for Exceptional Individuals, 30*(2), 92–103.

U.S. Department of Labor. (1992). *Secretary's commission on achievement of necessary skills.* Retrieved from http://wdr.doleta.gov/SCANS

Wagner, M., Newman, L., Cameto, R., Levine, P., & Garza, N. (2006). *An overview of findings from wave 2 of the National Longitudinal Transition Study-2 (NLTS2).* Menlo Park, CA: SRI International.

Wandry, D., Webb, K., Williams, J., Bassett, D., Asselin, S., & Hutchinson, S. (2008). Identifying the barriers to effective transition planning and implementation: A study of teacher candidates from five teacher preparation programs. *Career Development for Exceptional Individuals, 31*(1), 14–25.

Wehmeyer, M. L., Agran, M., & Hughes, C. (1998). *Teaching self-determination to students with disabilities: Basic skills for successful transition.* Baltimore, MD: Brookes.

Wehmeyer, M. L., Field, S., Doren, B., Jones, B., & Mason, C. (2004). Self-determination and student involvement in standards-based reform. *Exceptional Children, 70*(4), 413–425.

Wood, W. M., Karvonen, M., Test, D. W., Browder, D., & Algozzine, B.(2004). Promoting student self-determination skills in IEP planning. *Teaching Exceptional Children, 36,* 8–16.

PART II

PRACTICES IN COMMUNITIES

CHAPTER 4

THE DEVELOPMENT OF GRASSROOTS NETWORKS FOR LATINO FAMILIES OF CHILDREN WITH DISABILITIES

Michael P. Evans

INTRODUCTION

Just before lunchtime, Eva is preparing for an important meeting when she receives a call at her desk. Her third-grade daughter has a fever and needs to be picked up from school. Hanging up the phone, she quickly places a call to her mother-in-law with the hope that she will be able to help care for the child.

Around the world, millions of similar scenarios occur each day. The African proverb, "It takes a village to raise a child" rings true, as evidenced by the numerous microinteractions that are required to enable the care of a child. Additional support may be provided by family, neighbors, schools, healthcare professionals, or countless other community members. The image of the independent nuclear family has become outmoded as increasing evidence reveals that most families rely on complex interdependent

Promising Practices to Empower Culturally and Linguistically Diverse Families of Children With Disabilities, pp. 51–65

networks to help care for their children (Cochran, 1993; Dominguez & Watkins, 2003; Hansen, 2005). Networks have become an important part of most families' lives, but networks become even more essential to families of students with disabilities (Turnbull & Turnbull, 2001). Many families feel unprepared to support their child with disabilities, however, their involvement is important to their child's achievement. Family involvement has critical outcomes. Research indicates that students with disabilities who benefit from strong parental involvement are more likely to be closer to grade level, have higher rates of involvement in school activities, and achieve greater independence in the future (Barlow & Humphrey, 2012; L. Newman, 2004; Simpson, Peterson, & Smith, 2011).

Unfortunately, there are many barriers that culturally and linguistically diverse (CLD) families encounter when trying to support a child with disabilities. These barriers may include issues related to socioeconomic status, language, communication, and general power imbalances (Brandon & Brown, 2009; Geenen, Powers, & Lopez-Vasquez, 2005). Although the Individuals with Disabilities in Education Act includes a mandate for family and school collaboration, this mandate is frequently forgotten by many administrators working with culturally diverse families. These school leaders may have low expectations for CLD families, so the priority becomes simply making sure that parents or guardians attend individualized education programs and sign the necessary paperwork (Kalyanpur, Harry, & Skrtic, 2000). A recent study of urban families in the Midwest found that accessing networks does improve a CLD families' ability to support their child (Munn-Joseph & Gavin-Evans, 2008). The authors describe how parents used a combination of social networks (family and friends) and institutional networks (social service providers, healthcare workers, etc.) to gain information and advocate for their children. In particular, knowledge acquired from the institutional networks was used as "social leverage" to improve "social and material conditions" of the family (Munn-Joseph & Gavin-Evans, 2008, p. 389).

This chapter extends this research by exploring the experiences of several Boston-based families who were able to expand the effectiveness of their social networks through participation in a community-based organization that utilized community-organizing strategies. Community-based organizational efforts have grown throughout the past 20 years. This growth is a result of their overall effectiveness as a change strategy for the empowerment of families that have historically been excluded from education dialogues (Mediratta, Shah, & McAlister, 2009). Some key features of education organizing work include an emphasis on relationship building, leadership development, and a focus on collective action (Warren, 2010). The individuals described in this chapter were empowered by the education organizing process and created new multifaceted networks.

These networks allowed them to engage with institutional leaders and become more effective advocates for the children in their community.

RESEARCH METHODS

The data for this chapter comes from a larger ethnographic study examining the internal workings of three Massachusetts-based community-based organizations working on education issues. Data was collected from 2006 to 2008 and included formal interviews, observations, and document analysis. This chapter is based on the findings from the JP-POP case study. The JP-POP data included interviews with the lead organizer and eight community-based organizational members. Interviews were conducted with the help of a translator. Observations were conducted at training sessions, school board meetings, rallies, house meetings, and other special events. Finally, documents (agendas, brochures, fliers, etc.) were collected at the above events and included in the data analysis. All of the data underwent three stages of coding using an iterative process supported by the software program NVivo. Overarching themes were identified, and the findings related to the development of networks are reported below.

JAMAICA PLAIN-PARENT ORGANIZING PROJECT

The Haffenreffer Brewery has long been a landmark in the Jamaica Plain neighborhood of Boston and presently hosts a number of successful small businesses and nonprofits, including City Life/Vida Urbana. City Life/Vida Urbana is a community-based organization established by political activists in 1973. The organization began to gain recognition through their successful efforts to block widespread evictions in the neighborhood and attempts to unify support for local desegregation efforts. Over the decades, housing and tenant rights have continued to be important issues for City Life/Vida Urbana, but they also continue to evolve to meet the needs of the community. Today, in addition to the Tenant Organizing Program, City Life/Vida Urbana also directs programs for first-time homebuyers, healthy families, Latino leadership programs, and, the subject of this chapter, a parent-organizing project.

In 2002, the JP-POP was formed as a subsidiary of City Life/Vida Urbana with a primary focus on education, in particular, the needs of bilingual learners and children with disabilities. Although membership in JP-POP is open to anyone, participants are primarily low-income, Spanish-speaking women representing the Boston neighborhoods of Jamaica Plain, Roslindale, Hyde Park, South Boston, Roxbury, and Dorchester. Annual membership dues of $30 are paid directly to City Life/Vida Urbana. JP-POP networks with other parent and advocacy groups in the city, but their core constituency remains predominantly Latino. This membership growth may be attributed to word of mouth by members because members are more likely to invite people from inside their own social circles. Membership is also drawn from referrals by other City Life/Vida Urbana programs like "Latinos Comprando Casa," in which most of the attendees are Spanish speakers. Most members have children with moderate to severe disabilities. The group has developed an expertise in this area, and several parents first become aware of JP-POP through recommendations from other parents or teachers who are concerned about special education services.

The majority of JP-POP members became involved through some combination of the following four factors. First, many were referred to the group through their social networks, including friends, family, and professionals. Second, JP-POP has earned a reputation as a quality resource for the families of students with disabilities, and this draws in a number of members. Third, several parents expressed a desire to become more involved in their children's education but faced obstacles grounded in cultural and linguistic differences. Finally, some members had unpleasant encounters with Boston Public Schools (BPS) and were motivated out of concern about the well-being of their children.

ACTION ISSUES FOR JP-POP

JP-POP addresses issues as they emerge in the community. In general, the group addresses the interrelated issues of bilingual education, disabilities, and access to power. Bilingual education was the first major action for JP-POP and helped create a strong base for future actions. Special education was quickly identified as an additional area of high need in the community. Finally, access to power is an overarching goal that relates to all of the issues that JP-POP seeks to address. Thus far, the majority of JP-POP's work has occurred in the context of the Boston Public School District. Providing a high quality education for students with disabilities is a challenge for many school districts and the Boston Public Schools are no exception. In fact, according to the 20 indicators outlined in the Massachusetts State Performance Plan for the Federal Fiscal Year 2005–2010, the city is lagging well behind the rest of the state. When the data for this research was collected in 2006–2008, the graduation rate for students with Individualized Education Programs (IEP) was only 36.2%, far short of the state target of 61.6%. The dropout rate (12.3%) and full inclusion rates of students in IEPs (30.1%) were also well below the established state targets. While BPS does perform well in some areas, like the development of IEPs in early childhood, it is evident that there is much work to be done in the area of special education (MDOE, 2006).

DEVELOPING GRASSROOTS NETWORKS OF CARE

While many individuals were brought into JP-POP through friends and family, their social networks continued to grow as they met and worked with other group members. While some personal friendships did develop, the majority of the new relationships are more aptly describe as instances of familial collegiality. Members are friendly and often know intimate details of one another's lives, but these relationships generally did not continue outside of JP-POP events. JP-POP places little emphasis on the development of individual relationships, and activities are more group focused. Many members are extremely proud of the cohesiveness of the group. One interviewee commented, "Because we are all different, live in different places. I can say that I know them and some of them are friendly … maybe I am not socializing with them, but as a group we are so together."

There is a significant amount of diversity within the group that might not be appreciated at first glance. While on the surface the networks forged in JP-POP might appear to be primarily creating "bonding" forms of social capital (homogenous and inward looking), there are a number of important differences that allow "bridging" social capital to also be formed (Gittell & Vidal, 1998). For example, the children of JP-POP members might be broadly categorized as Latino or Hispanic by the school system for the purposes of demographic reporting, and school leaders might characterize some of these families as Spanish-speaking, but these broad labels fail to recognize how the ethnic origins of the members are important aspects of their identities and inform their interactions with schools. Members of JP-POP hail from the Dominican Republic, Puerto Rico, and Mexico, and there are other important differences, including the traditions that they honor and how they understand the role of school. For example, one Dominican mother described very maternal relationships between students and teachers back home, whereas another Mexican mother detailed a much more formal dynamic in which the schools and families had very little interaction. Intergroup diversity is also based on the specific disabilities of the members' children. Parents whose children share a specific disability are bonded based on their experiences and the likelihood that they might run into one another at other "disability-specific" conferences or events. Among JP-POP members, a widely held belief is that the diversity of the group members helps create a stronger whole because of expanded access to various types of expertise.

THREE PRIMARY ASPECTS OF NETWORKS

The grassroots networks of care that develop provide members with a variety of different supports that can be leveraged into individual or collective action. There are three primary aspects of the network that were identified in the data: technical support, emotional support, and logistical support (see Figure 4.1). Technical support provided access to the formal knowledge base that allowed parents to identify best practices for supporting their children. Emotional support was the personal relationships that empowered families to carry on in the face of difficult circumstances. Finally, logistical support provided knowledge that helped members navigate the complex bureaucracies of a large urban school district. These network characteristics are not discrete categories; rather they are interconnected webs that collectively empower JP-POP members.

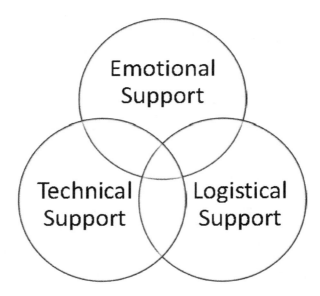

Figure 4.1.   Characteristics of JP-POPs' grassroots network of care.

Technical Support

Formal knowledge of education research and legal rights are a tremendous asset to members of community-based organizations. In this current era of accountability and high-stakes testing, there is an increased demand for research-based solutions to education issues. In order to effectively participate in policy dialogues, community-based organizations need to be well versed in the current research (Evans, 2011; Renée, 2006). Understanding a family's legal rights also allows them to more effectively advocate for their child. This sort of technical knowledge can be difficult for families to obtain, especially CLD families. JP-POP provides a framework that allows members to work together to gain collective technical expertise.

Members were eager to learn about pedagogical topics related to special education. In seeking to obtain information, half of the participants conducted research using the Internet, but the far more common means for acquiring this knowledge was participation in local workshops. Occasionally, JP-POP sponsored workshops in which the members selected topics and made all of the arrangements, including inviting speakers and advertising the event. Participants spoke about how accessible this training was in comparison to interactions at Boston Public Schools. Many parents are veterans of training provided by BPS and other social service agencies. Three of the participants recalled initially having some reservations about JP-POP, thinking that it would simply be more of the same. However, their skepticism quickly subsided when they discovered that the information was useful and empowering. As one mother remarked, "Before this, I was working with another agency, it was private and they do the things for you as an advocate, but they don't provide us with the tools. You see a person in the workshops [at JP-POP] and she provides us with the tools to do things for ourselves." The key difference was that members not only learned about the research, they were also empowered to use the research to help their children and themselves. Significant parent discussion during the JP-POP workshops focused on application of the research. The collective approach to understanding research and policy issues lent credibility to the information that was presented. One parent who had become exasperated with the bureaucracy of the school system was reinvigorated to face her child's challenges. She explained,

> Having other parents talk about their kids, to be honest with you, I feel renewed by the end of the meeting. They give good orientation, help you with what you need step-by-step. It is good because you get to learn and dialogue with one another. You learn so much about the services that you can get for your children at school.

Together, members figured out how they could best apply the research.

When other organizations hosted workshops, attending JP-POP members were responsible for collecting materials and sharing pertinent information with other members at the next meeting. While attendance at local events was important, much of the learning took place when members returned to analyze and digest the information together. The knowledge obtained through training was saved and adapted for future action and utilized as a shared resource. As a result, JP-POP had developed an extensive library of binders filled with information on a range of issues. The collection was particularly valuable because the information had been amended to reflect community knowledge. For example, a page describing a particular pedagogical approach might also include a notation with information about a local teacher who had direct experience using it in the classroom. These library materials had multiple levels of translation, including English to Spanish, technical jargon to layman's terms, and the addition of the aforementioned community knowledge. More experienced JP-POP members would also play an important role in helping to explain new concepts. One veteran leader noted,

> The learning process is hard. At the workshop last weekend, you could tell that it was confusing. For example, some of the parents heard (at the last meeting) that they could request one-to-one services. They were thinking that this would be like a personal tutor, but that is not the case. One-to-one is really intended for students with severe special needs or multiple handicaps. Even in these cases, it is not necessarily what is good for every student. It is important to make sure that everyone understands.

JP-POP members are able to benefit from the collective knowledge of the group and learn in an encouraging and supportive environment.

In addition to the research materials, JP-POP has also developed a series of training sessions to help support community members understand their legal rights. This technical information is especially helpful for immigrant families. "I am not from this country, so I don't know about the laws or all of the rights that the children have, so they [JP-POP] help me to learn about this," remarked one mother, "They are very clear with their explanations." Many of the training sessions are organized and done in concert with other professional organizations. For example, the introduction to advocacy training (essentially a primer on parental rights) is conducted with the EdLaw Project, organized by a group of lawyers working to ensure student rights and equitable education in the city of Boston. Members of JP-POP quickly use the information that they obtain and "translate" this information into a user-friendly format that is accessible to others. Faced with the vast size of the Boston Public School system and the range of challenges that special education poses, JP-POP spends a significant amount of time collecting information and staying up-to-date with district policies. Serving as a informational clearinghouse is not a typical "action" for a community-based organization, this service keeps JP-POP members involved in the system and allows them to mobilize quickly around any emerging issues.

Emotional Support

JP-POP members also reported on the value of meeting other families with children who had disabilities. The arduous battle to obtain services can be a grind, and the struggle can feel isolating to parents within the school community. This is particularly true when one is already confronting linguistic barriers. Participation in JP-POP allowed members to encounter others who had similar experiences. Individuals with similar concerns would become resources for one another, but just as important, they would also become sympathetic listeners. JP-POP members would often find new recruits at the grocery store, the community health center, or the laundromat. These parents wanted to share the positive experiences that they had with others. One parent described meeting a neighborhood woman while waiting in the health clinic:

> She really felt overwhelmed and I let her know what steps she should take [to get services] and I let her know that with time it is going to get better. I know how she feels. I feel like we can help her so I am trying to get her to go to the JP-POP meetings.

Members were so excited and relieved to learn about the rights that they never knew they had, they were eager to share this valuable information with others.

A number of participants expressed feelings of intimidation in their dealings with schools. Linguistic barriers and cultural disconnects were the primary basis of this fear. One of the primary benefits of participation in JP-POP cited by several members was an increase in confidence that allowed them to overcome their fears. This confidence is instilled in a number of different ways. Members became accustomed to public speaking on a small scale when they were asked to participate in the monthly meetings or at training sessions. The culture of support that the rest of the group provided helped those who are reluctant to participate even at this level. Preparation was another key element in building confidence. Members were well prepared in advance of meetings, and they are kept focused on the agenda, regardless of whether they are addressing a school board meeting or dealing with an IEP. The members became more self-confident because they knew what to expect in different situations. The knowledge that they gained regarding their personal rights was also an important factor. It enabled parents to assert themselves with educators, as one mother recalled,

> I used to be afraid to go to the school and I wouldn't talk to anyone at the school. But now that I know what my rights are, I realize that I need to speak up to advocate for my son. Before, I was afraid, but not anymore. A

few weeks ago I was at a meeting with my son's teacher and he [the teacher] called him [her son] a liar. I felt really insulted and after the meeting I sent my son out of the room and told the teacher how I felt. I said that his language was setting a poor example for my son who is trying to become less aggressive. The teacher acknowledged this and he actually apologized. I never would have done something like that prior to joining JP-POP. I would have been too afraid. I really feel empowered to speak up.

While JP-POP members are still deeply respectful of their children's teachers, they feel empowered to voice their opinion in a manner that many White, middle-class parents simply take for granted (Lareau, 2000).

One of the actions that JP-POP has become well-known for in the Boston Public Schools stems from knowledge that was gained in their legal training sessions. From the beginning, parents learned that families have the right to bring whomever they want to their child's IEP meetings. This has led to a practice in which multiple group members will attend IEP meetings with other JP-POP members as a sign of their support. Frequently, their presence is simply for the purpose of emotional support, but members will occasionally chime in with a question or comment. They always take the time to debrief after the meeting to discuss their impressions and next steps. Regardless of the level of involvement, the presence of the other members is always appreciated. As one new member remarked,

It's emotional because I'm talking about my child and I get very upset. My whole thing is, "Okay, why are you [the school] not trying to give her everything that she needs? Why are you trying to take things from her? You know what I mean? If she needs it and that's what your job is, why not give it to her?" It's emotional for me. It's like a power struggle, but these people are supposed to be here to help her, so it is nice to have the support of the others.

This practice has led to some unique situations in which community members will occasionally outnumber the teachers and administrators in the room, causing a significant shift in the traditional power dynamics of what is typically a daunting ordeal for many CLD families.

Logistical Support

Finally, the JP-POP network allows families to benefit from a range of logistical supports. For example, they have come to realize that their presence at various functions is critical in order to influence education policy. This was a revelation for some families. One mother from the Dominican Republic explained, "At home, there was very little interaction with the school because the teacher and parents trusted one another. A teacher at home is like another mother." This type of attitude is consistent with the research literature regarding many Hispanic immigrant families (Valdes, 1996), but it directly conflicts with cultural expectations in American public schools. However, attendance at school events is not always easy for working-class families. JP-POP works collectively to make sure that they are a presence in any important school or district meetings.

Of course, attendance is only one of the challenges that must be navigated for CLD families. For Spanish-speaking parents, access to school events, conferences, and meetings is severely limited. This is especially problematic at schools where there was not a large Hispanic population because it is less likely that someone can serve as an impromptu translator. One mother described her determination to demonstrate her commitment to her children's education despite being unable to communicate effectively in English:

> I have tried to get involved, and they say that they will get an interpreter, but when I show up at meetings, there isn't any interpretation available. It was only because I went in and asked for a school calendar that I learned about various meetings. I rarely get invitations to school events. Sometimes, even when I know that they will not have interpreters available, I still go to the meetings just so that they know that there are people who are willing to be present.

Observations of community—and Boston Public Schools—sponsored events confirmed the marked contrast in the participation of JP-POP members based on the availability of translation. For example, in January 2007, a community forum was held at the Freedom House in Roxbury regarding the hiring of a new superintendent. Among the standing-room-only crowd were members of JP-POP, proudly wearing BPON buttons (BPON was one of the organizers of the event). Translation was provided and Spanish-speaking attendees could wear headphones to listen to a simulcast of the event. JP-POP members were active participants in the event, and several made their way up to the microphone during the question-and-answer period to demand the continued participation of the community in the superintendent search process.

Several months later there was no translation provided at a special education conference focused on the transition of children from special education services to adulthood. Yet the members of JP-POP sat huddled in one corner of the Timilty Middle School gymnasium. One of the mothers, who possessed strong English comprehension skills, would whisper translations to the others during pauses in the talk. As the rest of the audience was drawn in and laughed with the energetic keynote speaker, JP-POP members strained to listen and understand. As one of the attendees later explained,

"It is very difficult because you have to focus so much on trying to under-stand the speaker. This makes it harder to listen to what they are *actually* trying to say. You end up missing a lot." However, the JP-POP members were present and they were able to participate because of the network that they had developed.

There are many other examples of logistical support within the organi-zation. For example, information about events and opportunities at various schools is passed between members. Because the participants' children are scattered throughout the schools, JP-POP keeps close tabs on what occurs throughout the district. Several of the participants also had relationships with people whom they trusted within the BPS system. These relationships were highly valued and provided "insider access" to information. As one member said, "I have a lot of resources in the community and I have a lot inside the Boston Public Schools. I have *my* people too. I have my connec-tions inside the Boston Public Schools and they help me be successful." There was tremendous appreciation for those insiders who were willing to go against the company line and recommend that members seek out a particular resource or even seek legal counsel. This was perceived as a sign that this individual had the true interests of the child in mind.

This local knowledge proved to be particularly helpful in a vast bureau-cratic system like Boston Public Schools in which contact with administrators often can be difficult. The members shared with one another how to navi-gate this complex system. For example, in one workshop, the guest speaker was listing the names of some individuals to contact at BPS. As one name appeared on the dry erase board, a JP-POP member said, "Oh, she never answers her phone. She is almost impossible to get a hold of." Another parent sitting across the room said, "Yes, but you can call Carol [a pseud-onym] who is in the office next door. Ask her to poke her head into the office and tell her to pick up the phone before you call." This type of infor-mation was acquired through experience and swapped freely among the parents. Collectively, the technical, emotional, and logistical supports that JP-POP members have cobbled together provide a powerful information network that supports CLD families and their children with disabilities.

CONCLUSION

Members of JP-POP received significant benefits from their participation in CBO activities. Through their expanded networks of care, they derived an increased sense of empowerment, proving that they did not need to rely on the beneficence of institutional insiders to support their children. This is a significant finding considering research indicating that schools often create feelings of inadequacy in CLD parents (Kalyanpur et al., 2000).

The members of JP-POP were able to simultaneously support individual members and contribute to broader systemic change. For example, in 2008 they successfully campaigned for the reallocation of $385,000 to support the hiring of six additional family-community outreach coordinators (Evans & Shirley, 2008). In was a substantial accomplishment in a climate in which funding was limited and an emphasis was placed on test preparation.

JP-POP's contribution to the family-community outreach coordinators campaign and their ensuing victory was celebrated by group members and school officials. This work also speaks to the potential for increased collaboration between schools and community-based organizations like JP-POP. Community-based organizations can be valuable collaborators and help bridge the family and school divide (Lopez, Kreider, & Coffman, 2005). According to two participants, their children's teachers specifically told them that as parents of a child with disabilities, it was important to learn about their rights and that they should "check out" JP-POP. This is compelling considering that JP-POP occasionally finds itself in opposition to schools and educators. According to JP-POP's lead organizer, these referrals are based on the fact the schools are overwhelmed, and despite occasional differences, they see JP-POP as a reliable source of information and assistance for families. However, research on community-based organizations also suggests that JP-POP possesses the ability to strike the delicate balance of agitating enough to compel change while maintaining legitimacy with school officials and decision makers who must implement reforms (Newman, Deschenes, & Hopkins, 2012).

Community-based organization members bring a valuable perspective to education debates, and they are motivated to work for sustainable change. These are the types of stakeholders that are needed to address broader educational issues and enhance the services that are provided to students with disabilities. For schools, it will require a commitment to reconceptualizing family-school-community relationships, but community-based organizations like JP-POP can become important contributors to the creation of an education system that meets the needs of all students and the broader community.

REFERENCES

Barlow, A., & Humphrey, N. (2012). A natural variation study of engagement and confidence among parents of learners with special educational needs and disabilities (SEND). *European Journal of Special Needs Education, 27*(4), 447–467.

Brandon, R. R., & Brown, M. R. (2009). African American families in the special education process: Increasing their level of involvement. *Intervention in School and Clinic, 45*(2), 85–90.

Cochran, M. (1993). Parenting and personal social networks. In T. Luster & L. Okagaki (Eds.), *Parenting: An ecological perspective* (pp. 149–178). Hillsdale, NJ: Lawrence Erlbaum.

Dominguez, S., & Watkins, C. (2003). Creating networks for survival and mobility: Social capital among African-American and Latin-American low-income mothers. *Social Problems, 50*(1), 111–135.

Evans, M. P. (2011). Learning to organize for educational change. In C. Hands & L. Hubbard (Eds.), *Including families and communities in urban education* (pp. 139–160). Charlotte, NC: Information Age.

Evans, M. P., & Shirley, D. (2008). The development of collective moral leadership among parents through education organizing. *New Directions for Youth Development, 116*, 77–91.

Geenen, S., Powers, L. E., & Lopez-Vasquez, A. (2005). Barriers against and strategies for promoting the involvement of culturally diverse parents in school-based transition planning. *Journal for Vocational Special Needs Education, 27*(3), 4–14.

Gittell, R., & Vidal (1998). *Community organizing: Builidng social capital as a development strategy.* Thousand Oaks, CA: Sage.

Hansen, K. V. (2005). *Not-so-nuclear families: Class, gender, and networks of care.* Piscataway, NJ: Rutgers University Press.

Kalyanpur, M., Harry, B., & Skrtic, T. (2000). Equity and advocacy expectations of culturally diverse families' participation in special education. *International Journal of Disability, Development & Education, 47*(2), 120–136.

Lareau, A. (2000). *Home advantage.* Lanham, MD: Rowman & Littlefield.

Lopez, M. E., Kreider, H., & Coffman, J. (2005). Intermediary organizations as capacity builders in family educational involvement. *Urban Education, 40*, 78–105.

Massachusetts Department of Education (MDOE). (2006). *School leaders' guide to the 2006 cycle IV accountability and adequate yearly progress (AYP) reports.* Malden, MA: Massachusetts Department of Education.

Mediratta, K., Shah, S., & McAlister, S. (2009). *Community organizing for stronger schools: Strategies and successes.* Cambridge, MA: Harvard Education Press.

Munn-Joseph, M. S., & Gavin-Evans, K. (2008). Urban parents of children with special needs: Advocating for their children through social networks. *Urban Education, 43*(3), 378–393.

Newman, A., Deschenes, S., & Hopkins, K. (2012). From agitating in the streets to implementing in the suites: Understanding education policy reforms initiated by local advocates. *Educational Policy, 26*(5), 730–758.

Newman, L. (2004). *Family involvement in the educational development of youth with disabilities. A special topic report from the national longitudinal transition study-2 (NLTS2).* Menlo Park, CA: SRI International.

Renée, M. (2006). *Knowledge, power, and education justice: How social movement organizations use research to influence education policy* (Unpublished dissertation). University of California, Los Angeles, CA.

Simpson, R. L., Peterson, R. L., & Smith, C. R. (2011). Critical educational program components for students with emotional and behavioral disorders: Science, policy, and practice. *Remedial and Special Education, 32*(3), 230–242.

Turnbull, A., & Turnbull, H. R. (2001). *Families, professionals and exceptionality: Collaborating for empowerment* (4th ed.). Upper Saddle River, NJ: Prentice-Hall.

Valdes, G. (1996). *Con respeto: Bridging the distance between culturally diverse families and schools*. New York, NY: Teachers College Press.

Warren, M. R. (2010). Community organizing for education reform. In M. Orr & J. Rogers (Eds.), *Public engagement for public education: Joining forces to revitalize democracy and equalize schools* (pp. 139–172). Palo Alto, CA: Stanford University Press.

CHAPTER 5

FAMILY SCHOOL PARTNERING TO SUPPORT NEW IMMIGRANT AND REFUGEE FAMILIES WITH CHILDREN WITH DISABILITIES

Gloria E. Miller and Vy Nguyen

NEEDS OF NEW IMMIGRANT AND REFUGEE FAMILIES

The U.S. school system is an influential source of support for families who have children with disabilities, but it is clearly an overwhelming and daunting system to understand for refugee families who have only recently entered the United States. A refugee is considered a person outside his or her country who is unable or unwilling to return to receive protection from that country because of persecution, or a well-founded fear of persecution due to race, religion, nationality, membership in a particular social group, or political opinion (BRYCS, 2012). There are no firm figures on how many refugee families resettle in the United States with children with special education needs.

Promising Practices to Empower Culturally and Linguistically Diverse Families of Children With Disabilities, pp. 67–84
Copyright © 2014 by Information Age Publishing

In America, parents are key decision-makers who collaborate with school professionals if a child is suspected of a delay or has a diagnosed disability. Family involvement is an essential and legally mandated component of the special education process (Ortiz, Flanagan, & Dynda, 2008). A strong family-school partnership based on respect for each other's values, beliefs, and expertise leads to a shared responsibility for a student's school success (Esler, Godber, & Christenson, 2008; Lines, Miller, & Arthur-Stanley, 2011). Students, regardless of age, social status, or ability, do better when families play an active role in their education (Christenson & Reschly, 2010; Epstein, 2005). Unfortunately, a host of challenges face refugee families when they enter the United States, which can seriously hinder the formation of strong family-school partnerships (UNHCR, 2002). This is unfortunate since schools have been identified as the most effective avenue for delivering a "system of support" to enhance the long-term success of refugee families and children (Kugler, 2009; McBrien, 2005).

While education is held in high regard, most refugees have limited experience and an incomplete schema of the daily expectations of school life. Researchers have pointed out important differences in the educational challenges faced by refugees entering the United States, in contrast to other culturally and linguistically diverse populations (Dow, 2011; Kia-Keating & Ellis, 2007; McCorriston & Lawton, 2008). First, refugee families often have had to wait a long time until they get word of a resettlement placement, and it is very common for children to go long periods without any formal education. Second, most refugee families and students have experienced oppression and severe trauma due to violence, war, flight, and loss, which can significantly affect brain development and interrupt learning, even when students have been schooled within their respective camps. These prior experiences can limit trust when dealing with authority and organizations like schools. Third is the fact that educational opportunities available in refugee camps are structurally, procedurally, and conceptually very different from Western educational systems. Fourth, refugee families and students may experience discomfort relating to persons they now live, work, play, and go to school with due to their limited exposure to diversity in the refugee camps.

Refugee parents often feel particularly insecure and uncertain about their role in their child's life once their child enters formal schooling in the United States (BRYCS, 2012). The considerable resettlement challenges faced by refugee families are compounded by the fact that educators consistently report that they are at a loss about how to engage refugee families in their child's education (Szente, Hoot, & Taylor, 2006). While researchers have begun to consider how to establish strong family-school partnerships with refugee families, much less is known about how to best accomplish this when refugee families have children with special education challenges.

THE COMMUNITY NAVIGATOR PROJECT

In this chapter, we review a new school-affiliated, community-based program designed specifically to empower newcomer refugee families to be partners in their children's education. The program, called the Community Navigator Project, is in its second year. The theory and rationale behind this program will be highlighted as will the promising first year outcomes. The components of this approach, while directed toward the educational needs of refugee families and students, may be applicable in fostering family-school partnerships with other newcomer culturally and linguistically diverse families who have children entering the special education system. Before this program is presented, key issues faced by refugee families who have a child beginning the special education process or already diagnosed with a disability are presented to provide a clearer picture of the significant hurdles that must be overcome when collaborating with refugee families who may have children entering the American special education system.

Family-School Partnering Issues Faced by Refugee Families

Overview

The issues presented below were identified through an ongoing interview study with refugee families who have been in the United States between 3 months and 2 years and who have at least one target child with suspected or documented disabilities. The children in this study had received little prior education and reflected disabilities such as autism, Down syndrome, traumatic brain injury, and cerebral palsy. Because the families had limited English skills and to establish a safe, supportive environment, all interviews took place at the family's home during one 2- to 3-hour session with a family-designated translator present. A semistructured open-ended, conversational interview was conducted, which consisted of four phases.

Initially, family members are invited to share their family story, with follow-up questions to gain a further appreciation of the family's culture, traditions, and hopes and dreams for their children. In the second phase, families discuss their overall impressions of the U.S. educational system, the challenges they have faced, and how it differs from their previous education experiences. During the third phase, the focus shifts to the family's views about the strengths and needs of their target child, and follow-up questions help to clarify beliefs and knowledge of their child's disability. The interview ends with a discussion of the special education system and questions to help clarify their expectations and understanding of the role they play in the special education process. (See the Appendix for a brief introduction to each phase.) Thus far, interviews revealed the same four areas of challenge by all five families who were interviewed. The credibility of these issues is bolstered by the fact that similar concerns have been consistently reported in other studies with culturally and linguistically diverse families who are learning how to navigate and support their child's education in the United States. The following are the four areas of challenge.

Supportive Relationships

A supportive relationship is one in which each partner feels understood and trusts that the other will go out of their way to help and follow through as promised (Lines et al., 2011). The refugee families we interviewed found it difficult to build such relationships with anyone at their child's school. Families often perceived staff members as too busy and rushed for time and in some cases felt that school staff were disinterested or had negative impressions about their family's culture (Harry, 2008; Kia-Keating & Ellis, 2007). In only one case had a family been asked to share their stories, values, or perspectives on how the American education system differed from what was experienced in the past (Collignon, Men, & Tan, 2001; Hughes & Beirens, 2007). Even though all families indicated a desire to form a relationship with someone at their child's school, none knew whom to go to for help or to advocate for their child (Hamilton & Moore, 2004; Kanu, 2008).

Welcoming Environments

Welcoming environments are created when families feel connected and perceive the school to be personally relevant, safe, and attractive (Lines et al., 2011). The refugee families we interviewed felt uncomfortable contacting teachers or visiting the school due to their limited English skills and not knowing if a translator would be present. Most families said they would feel better if educators were willing to come to their home or gave them a choice of meeting time and venue (Allen, 2007; Chu & Wu, 2012). Transportation concerns compounded by limited English skills were a barrier to navigating complex bus schedules required to visit their child's school (Collignon et al., 2001; Turney & Kao, 2009). In fact, one parent spoke of riding a bus all day not knowing where to get off and feeling afraid to ask for directions.

Two-Way Communication

Two-way communication occurs when family members and educators send and receive information from home to school and school to home (Lines et al., 2011). Such open lines of communication are best achieved through individual invitations to contribute, encouragement to ask questions, and when the initial focus is on a student's strengths and success

(Hiatt-Michael, 2010). Our families often reported participating in school meetings without any school facilitated preparation beforehand. Even when a school-appointed translator was present at a meeting, many families felt the material was presented very quickly, and they did not feel comfortable asking questions or sharing personal concerns about their child in front of strangers (Diez, Gatt, & Racionero, 2011; Harry, 2008). While all families desired more information about their child's performance, they also had not taken the initiative to volunteer in their child's classroom or set up an appointment to talk with their child's teacher(s). When asked to explain their hesitancy, family members voiced embarrassment about their English ability and also expressed a limited understanding of their collaborative role as experts regarding their child. These families were not expecting to be asked to give their opinion or ideas since they viewed educators as experts about their child's educational needs (Hamilton & Moore, 2004; Szente et al., 2006). These misperceptions clearly interfered with a family's ability to participate as a full partner in the decision-making process typically expected during team meetings with teachers and other school professionals (Roy & Roxas, 2011).

Educated Partners

Educated partners share cultural expectations and critical educational information so as to coordinate and support a child's learning at home and at school (Lines et al., 2011). Unfortunately, the refugee families we interviewed often had limited knowledge of their rights and responsibilities within the U.S. education system. Even though meetings and documents were translated into the family's native language, many key concepts were often misunderstood (e.g., terms like *confidentiality*, *progress monitoring*, *cognitive assessment*). While families had a strong desire to help their child with schoolwork, again they felt their limited education and English skills got in the way of this goal (Deslandes, Rivard, Trudeau, Lemoyne, & Joyal, 2012; Hughes & Beirens, 2007; Matuszny, Banda, & Coleman, 2007). Because of their unfamiliarity with what constituted a disability, our families did not feel they knew enough to make decisions for their child during special education meetings (Ortiz et al., 2008). Negative connotations about disability within their culture also were mentioned as barriers to collaboration (Okagaki & Bingham, 2010; Vazquez-Nuttal, Li, & Kaplan, 2006). In some communities, a child with a disability is considered a poor reflection on the family due to life choices or other family-related causes (Chu & Wu, 2012; Mitchell & Bryan, 2007). These impressions can lead to guilt, depression, and deflated feelings about being able to help their child learn (Jones, 2010; Kanu, 2008).

Summary of Critical Issues

Overall, our results mirror those found in many previous studies (Hill, 2010; Jones, 2010; Kanu, 2008; Kugler, 2009; McBrien, 2005; Vazquez-Nuttal et al., 2006). Refugee families need more opportunities to build relationships with key persons at their child's school. When refugee families have a student who is suspected of or is already identified with a disability, they not only need more specific information on their child's disability, they also need more guidance on their critical role in the special education process. In order to foster two-way communication about their child's strengths and needs, they need advanced preparation before team meetings and strong encouragement to give input, ask questions, and share their insights about their child and what they see at home. Refugee families also need practical ideas about what to do at home during daily life routines to make meaningful contributions to a support a child's learning. These results provide obvious ideas and advice to create more effective family-school partnerships.

The Community Navigator Project

Over the last decade, successful integration programs have been developed for refugee families that go far beyond the acquisition of linguistic competence to promote success in employment, education, health care, and housing. Community-based "newcomer programs" focus on building strong social networks within and outside their cultural community (Ager & Strang, 2008; Hughes & Beirens, 2007). Cultural brokers have been used to foster interaction between community leaders and families and to increase investments and reciprocity with community organizations (Yohani, 2013). While much has been written about how to help build a sense of belonging and a place in American society in general, less work has focused on the role of the public school in the acculturation process (Cooper, Chavira, & Mena, 2009; Gee, 2004) or on enhancing family engagement with their child's school. Yet in recent years, schools have been viewed as key to the development of a "system of local support" that can improve successful integration for newcomer families and students (DeJaeghere & Zhang, 2008; Karabenick & Clemens-Noda, 2004).

The Community Navigator Project (CNP) is a program specifically developed to promote family-school-community partnerships that foster greater family engagement in refugee students' education. The program was modeled on other successful programs designed to overcome barriers and improve the involvement of culturally and linguistically diverse newcomer families in their children's schools (Illinois State Board of Education,

2003; State of New York Education Department, 2010; Vazquez-Nuttal et al., 2006). Community navigators from similar linguistic and cultural backgrounds are trained as cultural brokers to facilitate collaboration between families and school professionals (Yohani, 2013). A focus on assets helps families, schools, and communities build upon resources that can support learning both in and out of school (Kugler, 2009; Matuszny et al., 2007; Mitchell & Bryan, 2007). Home visitation and monthly community family gatherings are critical to welcoming families and increasing awareness of educational expectations and opportunities (Suarez-Orozco, Onaga, & De Lardemelle, 2010). While these approaches have been successfully employed with immigrant and minority families, few have specifically focused on refugee populations (Diez et al., 2011; Dow, 2011; Singh, McKay, & Singh, 1999). The CNP was designed with this specific goal in mind.

Located in an urban, western city, the CPN began over 2 years ago with grant funding received from the state's resettlement and refugee services office. The goal of this grant was to develop a community-based, school affiliated program to increase refugee parent involvement in youth education and to improve relationships between local schools and their respective refugee communities. Home-school connections and family-school partnering were targeted as a basic means to improve the long-term success of refugee youth. The program was designed to address the educational challenges refugees face based on their unique experiences and unfamiliarity with the educational systems (BRYCS, 2012; McCorriston & Lawton, 2008) and founded on well-established principles of multicultural education, professional development, and community wraparound services (Allen, 2007; DeJaeghere & Zhang, 2008; Karabenick & Clemens-Noda, 2004; Turner & Brown, 2008).

The CNP is housed in one refugee-serving community agency, and the staff includes a project coordinator and nine trained community navigators who were former refugees representing the communities with whom they work. The navigators were recruited through public announcements, discussions with community agencies who serve refugee populations, and through word of mouth within the community. They receive a small monthly stipend to cover 25 hours of service to educate, advocate, and build strong family-school partnerships through informal home gatherings, meetings held at the school, or community outreach. The community navigators, who have been in the United States from 5 to 15 years, live in areas across the state where their Bhutanese/Nepali, Karen, Karenni, Mon, Chin, and Burmese, Eritrean, Congolese, and Somali families reside and have other full-time jobs or are enrolled part-time as college students.

The community navigators' major role is to encourage the participation of refugee families in their children's education. This is achieved by creating new avenues to promote a shared understanding of the American educational system and refugee-specific issues related to family-school partnerships. Once hired, the navigators receive over 20 hours of initial training followed by professional development sessions held every other month wherein they learn more about school-relevant programming and other key educational resources and programs. Community navigators, with input from the project coordinator, are responsible for planning monthly family meetings on community-relevant topics. The project director oversees all activities and provides weekly individual supervision and feedback as needed.

The initial training that the navigators receive focuses on critical schooling and partnership issues that they then are expected to "teach" to their assigned refugee families. These training topics were developed based on best practice in collaboration with a community advisory board composed of school district administrators and staff and community agency professionals who serve refugee impacted areas across the state. The training includes the following topics: "Understanding and Navigating the U.S School System," "School Rules, Discipline, and Procedures," "Absenteeism and Attendance," "Homework and Parent Involvement in the Home," Communication with Schools," "How to Become More Involved in Youth Education," "Communication with Your Child," and "What to do about Bullying."

The community navigators understand the challenges faced by newcomer refugee students and families as well as the curricula, activities, and resources at the school. While providing interpretation and translation is one aspect of their job, navigators view their major role as a cultural liaison who concentrates on fostering home-school collaboration within their respective communities to enhance students' success. They coordinate meetings and bring parents and teachers together to provide specific information on how to work together to help the child. They educate parents about the U.S. school system and teachers about families' respective cultures and point out similarities and differences between these two critical systems. Navigators help families understand the importance of participating in a child's schooling and encourage parents to ask teachers about classroom expectations, homework, and grading. Navigators are available to meet before, during, and after parent-teacher conferences or at other family-arranged meetings to share information and answer questions. They also encourage families to learn basic English skills and provide resources and other ideas to ensure this occurs. When asked, the community navigators say that they primarily provide emotional support and encouragement, which helps refugee families gain confidence about how to build a strong relationship with their child's teacher(s).

First Year Outcomes

Families were recruited into the program either though their assigned schools or by lists sent to the CPN agency by the state resettlement office. At this time, services have been provided to over 30 different schools across seven different school districts with services expected to expand during the second year of the project. First year outcomes were assessed through an examination of program inputs, resources, and outputs linked to quantifiable short- and long-term goals. Several program evaluation measures were developed to assess implementation success, including a community navigator professional development tool, a school staff/teacher feedback tool, and a tool to track all community navigator activities. Students' school records were examined, and surveys and interviews were conducted with school administrators, teachers, and families in the program as well as with the community navigators.

A review of the programming provided by the community navigators throughout the year indicated that initial activities primarily centered on building supportive relationships, introducing the program, and learning about the obstacles families were facing that prevented them from collaborating with their children's schools or becoming more involved in their children's education. By November, after the navigators held their first community workshops, efforts shifted to more specific activities designed to build bridges between refugee parents and teachers. Over the first year of the project, the community navigators in total delivered over 93 hours of family-school partnering education during monthly community workshops. Community navigators also attended routine parent-teacher conferences and many other meetings between a refugee parent and a school teacher/counselor. These efforts enabled 258 refugee families to learn more about their child's school, how to follow their child's academic progress, and how to support their child's education in a new country. Refugee parents made contact with their child's teachers 297 times, of which 92% were occasions in which the family went to their child's school or classroom. The majority of these meetings (i.e., 67%) were the first time a family made contact with their children's school. This proactive parent involvement resulted in a preventative, early intervention for a student on 30 occasions.

Focus groups conducted with participating families and the community navigators indicated that more families reported going to or initiating one-on-one meetings with their child's teachers after they participated in parent-engagement workshops run by their navigators. Refugee families also reported that they used more community resources to support student success, such as obtaining library cards and enrolling their children in summer education activities. A review of school records indicated that students in the program attended school at similar rates as other student populations at the school, and a higher percentage of families enrolled in the program attended parent-teacher conferences than families not enrolled in the program. Surveys completed by most families in the program indicated that over 80% of the respondents highly agreed that the CNP helped them gain a better understanding of the importance of parent-teacher partnerships in the United States and helped them feel more comfortable in their ability to communicate with their children's teachers. Over 90% of the families surveyed also agreed that the assistance received from the community navigators provided critical support, which increased their confidence in how to foster their student's education.

Other indicators of success related to overcoming common barriers faced by newcomer refugee families and students. With regard to relationships, families felt the project gave them an opportunity to build an initial connection with someone in the United States who understood their culture and who also knew how to make connections to key people at school. The navigators helped families gain trust in the schools by setting up informal as well as formal meetings between family members and school personnel. This led to enhanced working relationships that eventually fostered successful problem-solving between families and school staff when a student was having difficulties either at home or at school. Families reported they felt more confident and comfortable interacting with school members, and teachers felt they were more able to work with families to design learning strategies that could be used at home. The navigators also increased refugee families' participation in school activities and also mobilized community resources. These efforts fostered more positive attitudes toward refugees in general and helped teachers and community members to come together to support family-school partnership efforts for refugee families.

The navigators taught families about routine school policies and classroom procedures in the United States. For example, clarification often was needed about student behaviors viewed by teachers as helpful, assertive, or successful (i.e., asking questions, challenging ideas of teachers or peers) and typical classroom management adaptations that single out a student (i.e., reinforcement charts) since these were not always viewed favorably by refugee parents who respectively saw these actions as disrespectful or unhelpful because they "spoil" the child or single out the child unnecessarily. Time orientations also were clarified to help families understand the pressures of a school day and the need to make appointments in advance and to be on time. To give families a better appreciation of what a school day was like, teachers were encouraged to model and share videos of what happens during reading, math, lunch, recess, and such. Families also learned about their legal rights to services available in the United States, which included clear information about their role as active participants on educational teams who decide how to best support their child's success.

Navigators also alerted newly arrived refugee parents about opportunities to receive English-learning services. Finally, navigators regularly arranged meetings between refugee parents and teachers to discuss joint expectations and communication strategies and advocated with school administrators for services that would allow more refugee family members to attend school events (i.e., arranging for translators and babysitters, offering food and transportation).

Continuing Challenges to the Program

One major challenge faced during the first year of the CNP was the unanticipated district mandates that slowed down initial school programming efforts. The work that was completed in year one will help ensure that school outreach efforts will be more efficient and easier to generalize to other schools in year two so that more refugee families might be supported in the future. Another challenge was the limited time available for community navigators to consult with other family assistance agencies to clarify benefits, assist with job searches, or help with housing challenges. The navigators struggled with how much they could stray from school-engagement programming in order to meet other basic family needs. Next year, to avoid the expectation that community navigators can take on case management duties, more formal collaborative relationships, strategic planning, and professional development activities are planned with community agencies that can provide such services so that more holistic support can be offered to newly arrived refugee families to promote student success. Finally, another challenge was the limited time navigators had to devote to the project. Additional district funding is being sought that would allow navigators to spend more time collaborating with school staff to plan schoolwide professional development efforts that could increase educators' capacity to assist newcomer students and families entering the U.S. educational system.

Benefits of the Community Navigator Project

A consistent outcome associated with the CNP was that refugee families felt they had gained a better grasp of the U.S. school system and understood the importance of family-school partnering and its role in influencing their child's academic success. Families who feel more confident and welcomed at their children's schools will continue to gain experience partnering with their child's teacher (Vazquez-Nuttall et al., 2006; Wilkinson, 2002). It is likely that the initial relationships enhanced during the CNP will generalize to other educators as the child progresses and transitions across schools.

Another outcome was that educator beliefs and attitudes about refugee families changed (Hill, 2010; Karabenick & Clemens Noda, 2004). Teachers and administrators involved with the project reported on surveys and during interviews that they learned a lot about refugees in general and were more confident about partnering with refugee families in the future. These educators were especially appreciative of navigator assistance regarding student truancy and engagement issues, as reflected in the following comment: "My students seemed to be straying off track, but I saw this changing after I was able to communicate more effectively with their parents with the help of the navigator." Many teachers reported that refugee parents involved in the project began to volunteer more regularly in their classrooms and to ask more questions about assignments, which they linked to improvements in attendance and academic performance. Thus, this program may be a way to provide educators valuable cultural knowledge and insights that will help involve all newcomer families at their schools.

The critical lessons learned after year one are continuing in year two with the addition of several new strategies. To reach out to even more refugee families and educators, the community navigators plan to invite school personnel to their monthly meetings to discuss topics of interest and relevance to their community. Efforts also are underway to fine-tune and expand upon the family engagement curriculum, to add more training regarding the special education process, to secure funding for more community navigators, and to improve the program evaluation methods to further demonstrate the impact of this approach. Several recommended practices can be forwarded based on our completed interview data and the CNP outcomes reported after the first year. These suggestions are summarized in Table 5.1.

CONCLUSION

The information provided in this chapter suggests that broader models of family-school-community collaboration are needed to serve refugee families who have recently entered the United States. School-affiliated community-based approaches that employ community navigators from the refugee communities can build upon family strengths and increase parents' understanding of their role and rights in the American educational system. Trained cultural brokers who know both the home and the school culture can foster family and teacher confidence about working together to ensure a child's success. While more research is needed to document best practices that can support refugee families' adjustment to the U.S. educational

**Table 5.1. Suggested Practices to
Enhance Family-School Partnering**

Build Relationships	Create Welcoming Environments	Two-Way Communication	Educate Partners
• Ask family members to share their views/beliefs surrounding education.	• Connect families with someone from their home country who knows the U.S. education system, and if possible who has a child with a disability.	• Allow flex time so school staff can go on home visits and engage in cultural sharing interviews.	• Teach families about staff roles and teachers about family roles.
• Show interest by listening to a family's personal journey to the U.S. and the hopes they have for their child.	• Provide families with travel assistance to attend school meetings and functions.	• Ask families about prior experiences and cultural traditions, and ask teachers to share educational experiences and classroom traditions.	• Offer joint training to teachers and families on key issues such as student evaluation and homework.
• Find ways to learn more about and to honor family cultural traditions and history (e.g., share food / recipes, customs, demonstrate a trade or craft, discuss a book, travel pictures).	• Develop a simple guide in the family's native language on how to use public transportation to get to a child's school.	• Send home video clips of classroom activities to familiarize families with classroom expectations and to demonstrate a child's ongoing progress.	• Visit with families before and after team meetings to prepare them for what to expect and to ensure full understanding of the special education process.
	• Give families options for when and where to meet and invite a family-selected interpreter.	• Help parents learn English with support from community resources.	• Develop a guide of terms used in school-based meetings in the family's native language.
			• Provide models and examples of work expected in the classroom and at home.

system and engagement in their children's education, key aspects of the community navigator project clearly have the potential to guide future practice, policy, and programming to enhance family-school partnerships with refugee families who have children with disabilities.

APPENDIX:
CULTURAL SHARING INTERVIEW

Phase 1

During this phase, find out more about the family's story and journey to the United States. The purpose is to understand what it was like for the family to resettle in the United States and to gain a further appreciation of the family's culture, traditions, and hopes and dreams for their children.

Thank you for taking the time to talk with me today. I would really like to learn about you and your family and would like you to share your family's story about coming to the United States. Please know that if there are topics that you do not want to talk about, it is OK to let me know and we can talk about something else. I also would like to learn more about how the United States compares to what you have seen and where you have lived in the past. Please feel free to ask me any questions too. I also would be happy to tell you more about myself or to share any information I might have about the U.S. education system.

Phase 2

During this phase, it is important to understand the family's overall impressions of the U.S. educational system, the challenges and successes they have faced within this system, and how it differs from their previous education experiences. The purpose is to compare/contrast what the family understands about education from the perspective of their home country and the similarities/differences they perceive about education in the United States.

Moving to another country must have been challenging, and it is amazing how far you and your family have come. One of the reasons for the interview is to learn about how you view education and what differences you have seen since living in the United States. I would like to hear about how school has been so far for you and your (son/daughter's name).

Phase 3

During this phase, it is important to get more information on family demographics and the history of the target child. The focus should largely be on perceived strengths and needs, with follow-up questions designed to clarify beliefs about "disability" as well as knowledge of their child's disability. We want to know how the family felt when they learned that their son/daughter was diagnosed with or suspected of having a disability.

Tell me more about (target child's name). What does he/she like to do with you at home? What have you found helps him/her learn best? I know that throughout the world, the word "disability" can have different meanings and I would like to know more about what your ideas are about this too.

Phase 4

During this phase, it is important to gather information that pertains to the family's perception about their relationships with staff at their child's school and their ability to communicate and understand critical information regarding their child's education. The goal is to clarify their expectations of the role they play in the special education process.

In the United States, families and schools work together to provide the best education for students. I would like to learn more about how welcome you have felt when you have gone to your son/daughter's school. What type of relationship do you have with the teachers and staff at your child's school? How often and how well can you communicate with them? How confident do you feel about what you can do to foster your child's education?

REFERENCES

Ager, A., & Strang, A. (2008). Understanding integration: A conceptual framework. *Journal of Refugee Studies, 21*(2), 166–191.

Allen, J. (2007). *Creating welcoming schools: A practical guide to home-school partnerships with diverse families.* New York, NY: Teachers College Press.

Bridging Refugee Youth & Children's Services (BRYCS). (2012). *Refugee children in U.S. schools: A toolkit for teachers and school personnel.* Retrieved from http://www.brycs.org/documents/upload/ageandgradeFAQ-3.pdf

Christenson, S. L., & Reschly, A. L. (Eds.). (2010). *Handbook of school-family partnerships.* New York, NY: Routledge/Taylor and Francis.

Chu, S. Y., & Wu, H. Y. (2012). Development of effective school-family partnerships for students from culturally and linguistically diverse backgrounds: From special education teachers' and Chinese American parents' perspectives. *Scholarly Partnerships, 6*(1), 25–37.

Collignon, F. F., Men, M., & Tan, S. (2001). Finding ways in: Community-based perspectives on southeast Asian family involvement with schools in a New England state. *Journal of Education for Students Placed at Risk, 6,* 27–44.

Cooper, C. R., Chavira, G., & Mena, D. D. (2009). From pipeline to partnerships: A synthesis of research on how diverse families, schools, and communities support children's pathways to school. *Journal of Education for Students Placed at Risk, 10*(4), 407–430.

DeJaeghere, J. G., & Zhang, Y. (2008). Development of intercultural competence among American teachers: Professional development factors that enhance competence. *Intercultural Education, 19*(3), 255–268.

Deslandes, R., Rivard, M. C., Trudeau, F., Lemoyne, J., & Joyal, F. (2012). Role of family, school, peers and community in the adaptation process of young immigrants. *International Journal about Parents in Education, 6*(1), 1–14.

Diez, J., Gatt, S., & Racionero, S. (2011). Placing immigrant and minority family and community members at the school's centre: The role of community participation. *European Journal of Education, 46*(2), 184–196.

Dow, H. D. (2011). An overview of stressors faced by immigrants and refugees: A guide for mental health practitioners. *Home Health Care Management & Practices, 23*(3), 210–217.

Epstein, J. (2005). *Development and sustaining research-based programs of school, family, and community partnerships: Summary of five years of NNPS research.* Baltimore, MD: Johns Hopkins University

Esler, A. N., Godber, Y., & Christenson, S. (2008). Best practices in supporting school-family partnerships. In A. Thomas & J. Grimes (Eds.), *Best practices in school psychology* (5th ed., pp. 917–936). Bethesda, MD: National Association of School Psychologists.

Gee, J. P. (2004). *Situated language and learning: A critique of traditional schooling.* New York, NY: Routledge.

Hamilton, R., & Moore, D. (Eds.). (2004). *Educational interventions for refugee children: Theoretical perspectives and implementing best practice.* New York, NY: Routledge Falmer.

Harry, B. (2008). Collaboration with culturally and linguistically diverse families: Ideal versus reality. *Exceptional Children, 74*(3), 373–388.

Hiatt-Michael, D. B. (2010). Communication practices that bridge home with school. In D. B. Hiatt-Michael (Ed.), *Promising practices to support family involvement in schools* (pp. 25–55). Charlotte, NC: Information Age.

Hill, N. E. (2010). Culturally-based worldviews, family processes, and family-school interactions. In S. L. Christianson & A. L. Reschly (Eds.), *Handbook of school-family partnerships* (pp. 101–127). New York, NY: Routledge.

Hughes, N., & Beirens, H. (2007). Enhancing educational support: Towards holistic, responsive and strength-based services for young refugees and asylum-seekers. *Children & Society, 21*(4), 261–272.

Illinois State Board of Education. (2003). *Involving immigrant and refugee families in their children's schools: Barriers, challenges and successful strategies.* Retrieved from http://www.isbe.net/bilingual/pdfs/involving_families.pdf

Jones, J. (2010). Culturally diverse families: Enhancing home-school relationships. *Communiqué, 38*(6), 1–6.

Kanu, Y. (2008). Educational needs and barriers for African refugee students in Manitoba. *Canadian Journal of Education, 31*(4), 915–939.

Karabenick, S. A., & Clemens-Noda, P. A. (2004). Professional development implications of teachers' beliefs and attitudes towards English language learners. *Bilingual Research Journal, 28*(1), 69–74.

Kia-Keating, M., & Ellis, B. (2007). Belonging and connection to school in resettlement: Young refugees, school belonging, and psychosocial adjustment. *Clinical Child Psychology and Psychiatry, 12*(1), 29–43.

Kugler, E. (2009). Partnering with parents and families to support immigrant and refugee children at school. *Center for Health and Health Care in Schools, 1*(2), 1–19.

Lines, C., Miller, G. E., & Arthur-Stanley, A. (2011). *The power of family-school partnering (FSP): A practical guide for school mental health professionals and educators.* New York, NY: Routledge.

Matuszny, R. M., Banda, D. R., & Coleman, T. J. (2007). A progressive plan for building collaborative relationships with parents from diverse backgrounds. *Teaching Exceptional Children, 39*(4), 24–31.

McBrien, J. (2005). Educational needs and barriers for refugee students in the United States: A review of the literature. *Review of Educational Research, 75*(3), 329–364.

McCorriston, M., & Lawton, A. (2008, November). *Hand in hand: A resource pack to help meet the needs of refugees and asylum seekers in secondary school.* London: UK: Refugee Council.

Mitchell, N. A., & Bryan, J. A. (2007). School-family-community partnerships: Strategies for school counselors working with Caribbean immigrant families. *Professional School Counseling, 10*(4), 399–409.

Okagaki, L., & Bingham, G. E. (2010). Diversity in families. In S. L. Christianson & A. L. Reschly (Eds.), *Handbook of school-family partnerships* (pp. 80–98). New York, NY: Routledge.

Ortiz, S. O., Flanagan, D. P., & Dynda, A. M. (2008). Best practices in working with culturally diverse children and families. In A. Thomas & J. Grimes (Eds.), *Best practices in school psychology* (5th ed., pp. 1721–1738). Bethesda, MD: National Association of School Psychologists.

Roy, L. A., & Roxas, K. C. (2011). Whose deficit is it anyhow? Exploring counter-stories of Somali Bantu refugees' experiences in "doing school." *Harvard Educational Review, 81*(3), 521–541.

Singh, N. N., McKay, J. D., & Singh, A. N. (1999). The need for cultural brokers in mental health services. *Journal of Child and Family Studies, 8*(1), 1–10.

State of New York Education Department. (2010). *A resource guide for educating refugee children and youth in New York State.* Retrieved from http://www.p12.nysed.gov/biling/docs/RefugeeGuideFinal9-10.pdf

Suarez-Orozco, C., Onaga, M., & De Lardemelle, C. (2010). Promoting academic engagement among immigrant adolescents through school-family-community collaboration. *Professional School Counseling, 14*(1), 15–41.

Szente, J., Hoot, J., & Taylor, D. (2006). Responding to the special needs of refugee children: Practical ideas for teachers. *Early Childhood Education Journal, 34*(1), 15–20.

Turner, R. N., & Brown, R. (2008). Improving children's attitudes toward refugees: An evaluation of a school-based multicultural curriculum and an anti-racist intervention. *Journal of Applied Social Psychology, 38*(5), 1295–1328.

Turney, K., & Kao, G. (2009). Barriers to school involvement: Are immigrant parents disadvantaged? *The Journal of Educational Research, 102*(4), 252–271.

United Nations High Commissioner for Refugees (UNHCR). (2002). *Refugee resettlement: An international handbook to guide reception and integration.* Retrieved from www.unhcr.ch

Vazquez-Nuttall, E., Li, C., & Kaplan, J. (2006). Home-school partnerships with culturally diverse families: Challenges and solutions for school personnel. *Journal of Applied Psychology, 22,* 81–102.

Wilkinson, L. (2002). Factors influencing the academic success of refugee youth in Canada. *Journal of Youth Studies, 5*(2), 173–193.

Yohani, S. (2013). Educational cultural brokers and the school adaptation of refugee children and families: Challenges and opportunities. *International Journal of Migration and Integration, 14,* 67–79.

CHAPTER 6

COMMUNITY SUPPORT FOR PARENTS OF YOUNG CHILDREN WITH DEVELOPMENTAL DISABILITIES

Dana Kalek

SUPPORT FOR PARENTS

In the United States, 17% of the children have a developmental disability (Boyle et al., 2011). The term *developmental disability* refers to a severe and chronic disability that is attributable to a mental or physical impairment that begins before individual reaches adulthood (CDC, 2013). These disabilities include mental retardation, cerebral palsy, epilepsy, autism spectrum disorders, and conditions that are closely related to mental retardation or requiring similar treatment. In addition, many children with a developmental disability have delays in language, whether expressive or receptive, that impact development as well. The importance of early childhood prevention and early intervention programs is based on the premise

Promising Practices to Empower Culturally and Linguistically Diverse Families of Children With Disabilities, pp. 85–94
Copyright © 2014 by Information Age Publishing

that the first few years of a child's development are crucial in setting the foundation for lifelong learning, behavior, and healthy outcomes (Gauntlett, Hugman, Kenyon, & Logan, 2001).

Therefore, an early intervention program for parents of young children with developmental delays was developed to provide support to parents and their child. This chapter describes this program and its benefits to parents and their children. Evidence has emerged from a wide research base in health, developmental psychology, neuroscience, education, and criminology about the importance of promoting positive family and community experiences for young children during the earliest years of childhood (Pelchat & Lefebvre 2004; Shacar, 2006; Shonkoff & Phillips, 2000). Having parents who are able to provide children with positive experiences throughout childhood is important. However, this may be difficult for parents of children with developmental disabilities, due to the amount of stress they experience, as they have been observed to be less responsive to their children than are parents of children without disabilities (Estes et al., 2009; Mahoney & Powell, 1988).

PROBLEMS FOR PARENTS WITHOUT SUPPORT

Parents of children with disabilities often experience depression, anxiety, and low self-esteem due to the significant amount of stress accompanied with dealing with a child who has an array of delays. This is especially evident with parents of children with developmental disabilities, lifelong disabilities that require intensive therapeutic services (Tobing & Glenwick, 2002; Woolfson & Grant, 2005). These parents report higher levels of stress, especially with respect to feeling that their child is more distractible, more demanding, not measuring up to their expectations, and less adaptable in society. Parents have to cope with many uncertainties about their child's health and prognosis, frequent medical appointments and procedures, and the additional workload of caring for a child with a disability. Zelkowitz, Bardin, and Papageorgiou (2007) examined anxiety and stress of 88 families following the birth of a very low birth weight infant for 2 years. They found that all parents experienced increased distress following the birth of premature infant.

Higher levels of stress, anxiety, and depression can have a negative impact on parenting (Foley & Hochman, 2006; Koegel & LaZebnik, 2004; Singer et al., 1999). The psychological distress of parents of children with developmental delays can impact the development of parent-infant relationship. Guralnick (2000) believes that parent-child transactions normally include contingent responding, reciprocity, affective warmth, and providing developmentally appropriate challenges. If these interactions are interrupted, the quality of parent-child interactions is altered, and the parent's ability to build an ideal affective relationship with their child is vulnerable, ultimately effecting the child's development. Therefore, the Child Development Institute (CDI) was created to provide an early intervention center for parents as well as children.

THE CHILD DEVELOPMENT INSTITUTE

Mission

The CDI is a nonprofit family-centered early intervention center located in the San Fernando Valley, California. The CDI focuses on the development of the whole child, including his or her early relationships, environments, and communities through a relationship based model. The mission of the CDI is to help children with developmental disabilities, ages 0–8, in reaching their full potential by supporting the relationships and environments that shape their early development. This mission is built upon Bronfenbrenner's (1979) ecological system as well as the developmental systems approach to early intervention by Guralnick (2005). In an effort to empower, inform, and support the parent-child relationships, the program offers clinical-based, home-based, as well as community-based therapy to young children with developmental disabilities and their families.

This nonprofit serves approximately 300 middle- to upper-class English-speaking families of children with developmental disabilities and provides their children with free therapeutic services. Each year, the CDI receives funding from private foundations, regional centers, as well as nonpublic agencies. Additionally, fundraising events occur throughout the year for funding support. The CDI has approximately 80–85 staff members, including psychologists, marriage and family counselors, mental health interns, child development specialists, occupational therapists, speech therapists, school-age coordinators, program managers, and administration staff. All staff members work collaboratively to ensure that the children and families they serve receive quality multidisciplinary services.

Family-Focused Relationship-Based Model

Overview of Services
Early intervention services must include the needs of the entire family, not just the developmental needs of the child. The rationale for this emphasis is that the family is the most influential and constant factor in a young child's development and as such has the greatest impact on the child's

ability to reach his or her developmental potential (Shonkoff & Phillips, 2000). Therefore, the CDI is aimed to work with families, ensure parent participation, address family needs, and include families as potential recipients and beneficiaries of services. The CDI provides an interdisciplinary therapeutic approach to meet the individual demands of each child and family. Services are provided based on the individualized needs of the child and the family and are delivered in the home, in the center, or in the community.

When new parents begin participating in the CDI, they are required to meet with a lead specialist, who is familiar with child development, and are informed of the center's philosophy, rationale of treatment, and the various interventions available. After the initial meeting, parents meet with their assigned lead therapist individually on a weekly basis to review the types of support the child and parents need. Before their children receive floortime therapy, parents are encouraged to attend floortime training workshops. These workshops give parents background information on the floortime approach as well as to discuss individual, sensory, and speech and language needs of children. Details of each type of services that is provided by the CDI are discussed in the following sections.

Floortime Therapy

Floortime therapy refers to getting down on the floor with the child and engaging him/her in play to organize regulation, attention, and engagement; increase two-way communication; and develop representation of experiences. Floortime is a systematic way of working with a child to develop an improved emotional connection to caregivers. Once established, this relationship will serve as the basis for helping the child master the presymbolic stages that will develop into language and other higher level symbolic capacities. Hence, the parent involvement in floortime is the first therapeutic goal in which the parent's job is to follow the child's lead and play with whatever is capturing the child's interest at the time in an effort to initiate and sustain engagement (Greenspan & Wieder, 1998). Depending on the child's needs, s/he can receive floortime therapy from 2 hours to 20 hours per week.

Speech Therapy

The speech therapists at the CDI work with children and their families to enhance and develop language skills. In addition to speech and language therapy, speech pathologists provide feeding evaluations as well as feeding therapy to children who present with feeding issues. Techniques and goals developed by speech and language therapists are aimed at increasing the child's individual interest and ability to learn language. Parents are required to participate in the therapy sessions and implement learned strategies in the home to further help their child's language development. Additionally, if the child receives speech therapy at the school district, ongoing communication between the speech therapist at the CDI and the one at school occurs frequently.

Occupational Therapy

The CDI's occupational therapists work with children and their families through a family-centered approach in which parents are an integral part of therapy and involved in the weekly sessions. The focus of therapy is on the child's sensory, fine, and gross motor domains. Additionally, activities of daily living that include the child's ability to perform the tasks needed for self-care (i.e., grooming, oral hygiene, bathing, dressing, feeding, etc.) are addressed. All therapies are provided through the context of play wherin the expertise of the occupational therapist is used to assist the child in playing as a means of self-expression and fun, and as a means of assisting parents to strengthen their interaction with their child. Direct communication between the occupational therapist working with the child at the CDI and the occupational therapist working with the child in the school setting occurs to enhance child's progress.

Mental Health Therapy

In addition to the above therapies, the CDI offers parents the opportunity to attend individual mental health counseling with a psychologist or a licensed marriage and family therapist in an effort to provide the parent with opportunities for additional support. The effect of a child's diagnosis on a parent can be profound, and the child's lifelong difficulties may pervade the marriage, siblings, and extended family members.

Social Skills Groups

Social skills groups are an important component of the CDI's early intervention center. The groups are staffed one-to-one, with each child having their own therapist for the duration of the session. Each group meets for 2 hours. Participated children are usually placed in groups according to their developmental level. Groups meet anywhere from once to twice a week. The goal of the social skills groups is to allow children the opportunity to engage with others while remaining regulated by using the floortime principles as guidelines. Therefore, following the children's lead and looking for opportunities to encourage interactions are a key component. These social interactions between the children are facilitated by the therapists. Additionally, group leaders create specific opportunities that motivate children to work together wherein discussions and interactions are encouraged and supported. Another important goal of the social skills group is to encourage positive separation from the parent. Therapists work closely with parents to enable the child to separate from his/her parents while maintaining a calm regulatory state. For children who have a more difficult time in this process, a therapeutic plan is developed with their parents and implemented to encourage successful separation based on the individual needs of the child.

Parent Support Groups

Because of the emotional turbulence and increased stress levels experienced by many parents of children with developmental disabilities, it is imperative that families receive support to endure the process. The CDI functions within a strength-based model in which building resilience and confidence in parents in order to empower and help them navigate and cope with whatever lies ahead is crucial. As such, the CDI offers parent support groups that meet weekly for 2 hours. The parents meet during the same time that their children are in the social skills group. Each group consists of no more than six parents. All groups are led by psychologists, marriage and family therapists, and/or child development specialists. The discussed topics are based on the individual needs of the parents. As such, each parent brings their issues, their stories, their struggles, or their triumphs to share or discuss during group meetings. This form of support enables parents to develop strong friendships. Many of them continue to stay in touch even after their children no longer receive services in the CDI.

IMPACT OF THE CDI PROGRAM

Evaluation Study

To evaluate the effectiveness of the CDI on parents' level of stress, Kalek (2008) interviewed 30 parents who received a combination of therapies from the CDI for a minimum of 6 months. Nine guiding questions were used to determine what was and was not effective during their time spent at the CDI, such as "How has the program helped you obtain the knowledge and skills needed to feel comfortable taking your child out into the community?" The parents indicated that their children's problem behaviors had reduced after receiving services at the CDI. One mother of a 32-month-old child said,

> When we started, I had shame ... we were having lots of tantrums and she would throw herself down crying, screaming, and everyone was looking at me and thinking why couldn't I control my kid. It was a nightmare. My daughter has changed a lot. It was a nightmare going with her to the grocery store. Sometimes it would be 2 or 3 hours later and she would be screaming in the grocery store and I would call my husband to come from Simi Valley

to get her. I was crying and she was so upset and people were looking at me
… I can't say which therapy helped but she's changed a lot and the therapists
gave me tools…. Yes, I know what to do now.

Major Findings

Supportive Therapists

A total of 28 of the parent participants felt that their therapists provided
them with the most support as well as empowered them by increasing their
knowledge and information. Parents mentioned that their relationship
with their therapists was a significant highlight of the program. They felt
that they had someone to speak with and someone to listen to their feelings
and concerns while being in a safe and nonjudgmental environment. One
parent of a 22-month-old child said,

> I talked to my therapist once a week. I had a parent support session for 45
> minutes and that was really helpful. It was a time when she just listened and
> I could vent. We could reflect on what we had done that week. It was a time
> for me, it wasn't a family member it was just a third party that knows my son
> and that can support me. So I found that really helpful. But all the thera-
> pists were so encouraging and supportive. I would say the best part was the
> people, the personal relationships.

Stronger Family Relationships

And 27 of the participants stated that the program helped increase positive relationships within their family as well as strengthened their marital
relations. During their 6–18-month participation at the CDI, none of the
participating families separated from their spouse or commented on stressful marital relations. One mother of a 28-month-old child said,

> I think the program helped a lot because my husband and I were arguing a
> lot at the beginning of this process. And then I could ask the therapist how
> to explain what's going on to other people, help me explain the services that
> my son was getting. They would help me with that by suggesting responses
> that I could give to people instead of not knowing what to do. But now he
> knows what's going on and whenever he has the time he comes down here so
> he can see, and he likes it now…. With my mother coming it helped her to
> see … they get to see how the sessions are handled and learn how to speak
> to my kids.

Another mother of a 24-month-old child said,

The program absolutely made a difference. I think just having that support and being able to go somewhere that understands what this is all about is a big deal ... I was able to talk to my therapist about some frustrations so I was able to approach him [husband] differently and maybe get a better reaction and not make him feel like ... you know, he works a lot so I think that there's a lot of guilt. He is not there and he feels out of the loop. So instead of me being angry at him for not knowing, I was able to come home and share as much as I could and help him, show him and get him more on board. It has helped. I helped him understand me better. \

Successful Community Outings

Some 25 of the participants felt that the program provided tools and strategies to help them deal with their child in the community or natural environment. Parents stated this to be a significant concern during their start in the program as they felt "trapped" in their home and were unable to bring their child to the community due to their child's aggressive behaviors. A mother of a 30-month-old child said,

Oh gosh, the restaurants. I would totally avoid that. He would tantrum and want to do his own thing. I learned a lot of things from here to become a better parent for him.... I learned a lot of parenting skills and developmentally appropriate things. Now it is so much easier because I have the tools and know what to expect. Just knowing what he is ready for and what he is not ready for is really important.... I learned a lot all from bringing him here and from the therapists.

CLOSING THOUGHTS

Parents of children with developmental disabilities experience considerably high levels of stress. It is essential that parents are provided with support and understanding of the entire family system to strengthen family relations and build a stronger base for the child. The CDI clearly supports the needs of these parents. First, a family-centered early intervention center using a relationship-based approach strongly benefits families of children with developmental delays. Second, individual support to parents to increase their knowledge and empower them in their role so they are better able to navigate the daily struggles and stressors of having a child with significant developmental delays is crucial. Third, training early intervention staff to recognize the family as central in the development of the child while emphasizing the principle that all growth and development take place within the context of relationships is vital. In the future, the CDI plans on continuing and sharing this model with others throughout the Los Angeles County area in an effort to support children with developmental disabilities and their families in reaching their optimal development.

REFERENCES

Boyle, C. A., Boulet, S., Schieve, L., Cohen, R. A., Blumberg, S. J., Yeargin-Allsopp, M., ... Kogan, M. D. (2011). Trends in the prevalence of developmental disabilities in US children, 1997–2008. *Pediatrics, 127*(6), 1034–1042.

Bronfenbrenner, U. (1979). *The ecology of human development.* Cambridge, MA: Harvard University Press.

Center for Disease Control and Prevention (CDC). (2012, July 12). *Child development.* Retrieved February 13, 2013, from http://www.cdc.gov/ncbddd/childdevelopment/screening.html

Estes, A., Munson, J., Dawson, G., Koehler, E., Zhou, X., & Abbott, R. (2009). Parenting stress and psychological functioning among mothers of preschool children with autism and developmental delay. *Autism the International Journal of Research and Practice, 13*(4), 375–387.

Foley, G. M., & Hochman, J. D. (2006). *Mental health in early intervention.* Baltimore, MD: Paul H. Brookes.

Gauntlett, E., Hugman, R., Kenyon, P., & Logan, P. (2001). *A meta-analysis of the impact of community-based prevention and early intervention.* Canberra, Australia: Commonwealth Department of Family and Community Services.

Greenspan, S., & Wieder, S. (1998). *The child with special needs.* Reading, MA: Perseus.

Guralnick, M. (2000). Early childhood intervention: Evolution of a system. *Focus on Autism and Other Developmental Disabilities, 15*(2), 68–83.

Guralnick, M. (2005). *The developmental systems approach to early intervention.* Newtown, PA: Paul H. Brookes.

Kalek, D. (2008). The effectiveness of a family-centered early intervention program for parents of children with developmental delays ages 0–3. Malibu, CA: Pepperdine University.

Koegel, L. K., & LaZebnik, C. (2004). *Overcoming autism.* New York, NY: Penguin.

Mahoney, G., & Powell, A. (1988). Modifying parent-child interactions: Enhancing the development of handicapped children. *Journal of Special Education, 22*(1), 82–96.

Pelchat, D., & Lefebvre, H. (2004). A holistic intervention program for families with a child with a disability. *Journal of Advanced Nursing, 48,* 124–131.

Shacar, A. (2006). *Parenting an autistic child: A qualitative analysis of parents' perceived needs.* Malibu, CA: Pepperdine University.

Shonkoff, J. P., & Phillips, D. (Eds.). (2000). *From neurons to neighborhoods.* Washington, DC: National Academy Press.

Singer, L. T., Salvator, A., Guo, S., Collin, M., Lilien, L., & Baley, J. (1999). Maternal psychological distress and parenting stress after the birth of a very low-birth weight infant. *Journal of the American Medical Association, 281,* 799–805.

Tobing, L. E., & Glenwick, D. S. (2002). Relation of the childhood autism rating scale-parent version to diagnosis, stress, and age. *Research in Developmental Disabilities, 23,* 211–223.

Woolfson, L., & Grant, E. (2005). Authoritative parenting and parental stress in parents of pre-school and older children with developmental disabilities. *Child Care Health and Development, 32*(2), 177–184.

Zelkowitz, P., Bardin, C., & Papageorgiou, A. (2007). Anxiety affects the relationship between parents and their very low birth weight infants. *Infant Mental Health Journal, 28*(3), 296–313.

CHAPTER 7

COMMUNITY ORGANIZATIONS SUPPORTING SPECIAL EDUCATION ADVOCACY WITH DIVERSE FAMILIES

Terese C. Aceves and Ignacio Higareda

The journey for any parent is to obtain resources necessary for his or her children to thrive now and in the future. However, the political debate is still about whether our children with disabilities have real value as contributing citizens and whether the financial investment in their care and their education is justified in an environment of strong competing interests and limited resources. As parents can tell you, this subliminal undercurrent plays out best behind closed doors of IEP meetings in the local school, or in case management meetings with service providers who are pressured by limited resources to act as if this is a game of 20 questions, where if you know what to ask for, maybe your child will get it. The most effective parent negotiators and system navigators have developed strong advocacy skills and keen English-language skills and full knowledge of the American educational system and processes. So what happens to families who are new to the United States, are non-English speakers, and have no understanding of our complex society and structures? (Fiesta Educativa Parent and Advocate, *Education for All*, pp. 63–64)

This material is reproduced with permission of John Wiley & Sons, Inc.

Promising Practices to Empower Culturally and Linguistically Diverse Families of Children With Disabilities, pp. 95–110
Copyright © 2014 by Information Age Publishing

Since the 1970s, special education law in this country has required professionals to collaborate with parents in the decision-making process related to the education of their child with a disability. Although the legal requirement recognizes parents as equal partners with educators and other professionals, the reality of this vision remains elusive for an overwhelming number of families and particularly for low-income, culturally and linguistically diverse (CLD) families (Harry, 2008; Shapiro, Monzó, Rueda, Gomez, & Blacher, 2004). As so effectively expressed by the parent advocate at the beginning of this chapter, these families require additional expertise to access and manage the educational services their children require. The current chapter provides an overview of the literature in this area, followed by a description of two community organizations and their work supporting primarily Latino families whose children receive special education services.

REVIEW OF THE LITERATURE

Numerous issues limit the involvement of CLD parents in the education of children and youth with disabilities. A majority of the literature has focused on the needs of Latino families and their ongoing struggles when supporting their children with disabilities. These struggles include poor communication with professionals regarding educational services, major differences in cultural perspectives regarding disability and parent-professional roles, and limited access to appropriate special education and community services (Blanchette, Klingner, & Harry, 2009; Harry, 2008; Langdon, 2009; Tejero-Hughes, Valle-Riestra, & Arguelles, 2008; Turnbull, Turnbull, Erwin, Soodak, & Shogren, 2011). Latino parents also experience difficulty accessing information, including receiving adequate interpretation services during parent-professional conferences (Harry & Klingner, 2006) and obtaining written materials at an appropriate level of English or native-language proficiency (Gomez Mandac, Rudd, Hehir, & Acevedo-Garcia, 2012).

Parents of children with disabilities who have greater access to cultural and social capital acquire more resources, whereas those with limited resources only struggle to gain such access. Cultural capital includes material resources and knowledge that influence the manner in which one functions. Social capital involves an individual's social networks with friends, professionals, and family members that provide access to a variety of benefits including better services (Bourdieu, 1986). Examples of Latino parents accessing specific cultural capital to advocate for their child with disabilities include demonstrating greater knowledge of IEP content, parental rights, and strategies for supporting a child with disabilities at home (Tejero-Hughes et al., 2008; Trainor, 2010). Accessing information continues to be one of the difficult obstacles faced by families, particularly those from diverse backgrounds (Erwin & Soodak, 2008; Lo, 2009; Zoints, Zoints, Harrison, & Bellinger, 2003).

Tejero-Hughes and colleagues (2008), in their study about Latino families of children with disabilities, reported that their parent participants wanted the school to provide them with specific strategies to support their child at home. Providing opportunities for Latino parents to strengthen these essential capital resources, including their understanding of special education services and programs, alongside with other parents of similar background and in their native language, may strengthen the knowledge and resources they can bring to their partnership with professionals and schools. Community organizations often have the ability to provide Latino parents with such supports, which allows them to make significant differences in the lives of their children with disabilities.

Community organizations are public service agencies, including nonprofit groups and faith-based organizations, that serve a particular community. According to Bronfenbrenner's (1986) ecological systems theory, the community serves as an important context for children's development. Within this framework, children's development has multiple and immediate influences or microsystems (e.g., home, school, community), including the relationships that take place between these systems (known as mesosystems). Like schools, community organizations can function as change agents by providing necessary resources for parents to support their children's learning and development (Weiss & Lopez, 2010). Unlike schools, community organizations may have a greater ability and flexibility (through special funding, program and staff expertise) to provide critical resources unavailable at local schools for low-income and immigrant families (Weiss & Lopez, 2010). Moreover, public schools may also benefit by establishing more direct, active, and ongoing relationships with community groups to access these same resources. Their work can facilitate parents and schools' support of children and youth with disabilities both at school and at home.

The remainder of this chapter outlines the work of two nonprofit community agencies, Fiesta Educativa, Inc., a parent support organization, and Learning Rights Law Center, a legal educational advocacy group. The chapter also provides useful practices that parents, teachers, administrators, and other service providers can implement specifically with CLD families of children with disabilities.

FIESTA EDUCATIVA, INC.

Fiesta Educativa, Inc., based in California with offices in Los Angeles, Orange County and San Jose, was initially founded in 1978 to inform and assist Latino families in obtaining services for their children with disabilities. Implemented by family members and professionals who recognize the need to provide assistance and advocacy to CLD families, Fiesta Educativa's mission seeks to embrace universal support toward the enhancement of the lives of persons with disabilities through a collaborative partnership of families, professionals, consumers, friends, and agencies (Fiesta Educativa, Inc., 2007).

During the 2011–2012 academic year, the third year of a 3-year training program, Fiesta Educativa organized a school-based parent education program for low-income, Spanish-speaking parents who had a child receiving special education services. The purpose of the training program was to provide families with immediate access to quality expert information within the community that otherwise would be difficult for parents to obtain due to lack of English fluency, transportation, or a general lack of awareness regarding local community supports and services. Fiesta Educativa contracted local bilingual specialists from a variety of community organizations to present information related to understanding special education rights, communicating effectively with the school and during the individualized education program (IEP) process, supporting children's social and behavioral skills at home, and obtaining resources and services in the community. Session presenters developed their own training materials based on the content of the session and needs of the site.

The training program involved two elementary schools, one middle school, two high schools, and one special education center, all within the same school district. The program was fully implemented, with each of the six sites receiving a minimum of six on-site classes for a total of 36 training sessions for 190 parents. The following sections describe Fiesta Educativa's collaboration with school sites and strategies for maximizing parent participation during parent trainings.

Strategies for Maximizing Community Agency-School Collaboration

Early Planning and Preparation

Fiesta Educativa's executive director and staff met with district and site administrators at the beginning of the year to discuss the training program, targeted audience, logistics, session content, staff participation, and to determine the most appropriate day/time for the training sessions. Sessions at each site were scheduled on the same day and time, once per week, for 6 weeks. Some sessions took place during the school day or in the evening based on the needs of the site. Meeting with administrators and staff was critical to the implementation and success of the program. These meetings allowed the agency and schools to finalize session content (see Content Needs Assessment for details) and determine how best to contact families (see Targeted Parent Outreach section for details). This planning assisted the agency in understanding the structure and needs of the school site and determining how each school supported its Spanish-speaking families of children with disabilities. Some schools had very little if any ongoing support for these families. For example, one school hoped its collaboration with Fiesta Educativa would jump-start its parent involvement, which was quite inactive and negative in recent years. Another school had a very organized, preexisting parent program for all families. The principal enthusiastically offered 6 weeks of her scheduled professional development as possible volunteer hours for families to attend Fiesta's parent training. Finally, in order to better target the needs of each school site, the agency and school discussed the particular needs of their special education population, as the needs of students and families could differ greatly across sites (e.g. elementary versus secondary sites, and students with mild-moderate versus moderate-severe disabilities).

Content Needs Assessment

Session presentations initially addressed topic areas identified by the community agency as essential in its previous work with diverse special education families within the community. In order to confirm these topic areas and determine if additional topics needed to be addressed, the agency administered a needs assessment to school staff. These results were then discussed with the school administrator. Most areas identified by school staff fell within the topic areas previously identified by the agency. Additional topic areas identified by school sites were covered during bonus sessions. Bonus session topics included supporting students with autism, conservatorship, postsecondary academic and employment options, and Social Security Income (SSI) benefits. Parents from participating school sites were invited to attend bonus sessions at any school site.

Co-Facilitated Training Sessions

In order to promote greater parent participation and site implementation, the agency asked special education teachers to indicate during the early planning stage whether or not they could co-facilitate training sessions. These sessions would involve a presentation by an external expert trainer from the field on a session topic while allowing a school specialist to provide additional site-based information. The agency offered to pay for teacher substitutes if a training session conflicted with their work schedule. Given that trainings were conducted in the parents' primary language, it was also important to ensure that school staff could develop and deliver training sessions in Spanish. For monolingual English-speaking staff presenters, the agency requested schools to make arrangements for a bilingual interpreter to assist them. Joint sessions would allow parents to better understand the application of session content to their school site. Co-facilitated sessions would also encourage greater parent participation across sessions.

School Site Representation

In order to increase greater visible collaboration between Fiesta Educativa and school sites, Fiesta encouraged sites to identify a staff member (e.g., administrator, counselor, special education teacher, parent outreach coordinator) to attend regular training. Session attendance by a representative from the school was also intended to assist families to understand content and recommendations made by external speakers from the school's perspective. During previous implementation years, administrators suggested wanting greater presence during training sessions in order to avoid unintended confusion regarding the school's support for students with disabilities and their families. Site administrators who regularly attended training sessions openly offered suggestions and answered parents' questions. Moreover, parents viewed the attendance and participation of school staff and administrators during training as supportive. Their presence made parents feel as though their needs and concerns regarding their children's education were a priority for the school.

Strategies for Maximizing Parent Participation During Training

Parent Needs Assessment

Scheduling training sessions was done primarily during the initial planning meetings with site administrators and staff. However, it was necessary to send an additional needs-assessment to families of children with disabilities at the two participating high schools, given the challenge of encouraging parent attendance at those sites. School staff reported experiencing great difficulty in persuading parents to attend regular school functions (e.g., parent-teacher conferences). Special education families at two secondary sites reported wanting sessions to be provided over 1 or 2 weekends as a training conference in order to minimize the number of school visits required to participate in the program. Administering a needs assessment with school site families regarding their suggestions for topic areas would also help ensure that training content addresses families' particular needs and concerns.

Parents as Trainers

For a second year, Fiesta Educativa successfully integrated parents of children with disabilities as trainers for presentation sessions. Several invited speakers from local agencies, including Fiesta Educativa staff, were also parents of a child with a disability. These parents were able to openly share useful information, including their personal journey in supporting their own child with a disability. This authentic voice resonated with participating parents, given their shared experiences and the ability of parent trainers to provide reassurance regarding postsecondary outcomes for their own children. Parent trainers also shared how their knowledge, skills, and experience gained in advocating for their children transferred to career and employment opportunities. Participating parents shared that presenters understood their experiences and needs, demonstrated a sense of compassion and caring, and provided useful information related to special education services and supports.

Targeted Parent Outreach

Over the 3 years, encouraging parents to attend training sessions became critical during the preparation and planning stage. Fiesta Educativa, school administrators, and staff discussed at length a variety of strategies to encourage parent participation. School sites sent automated phone blasts and mailed bilingual flyers, prepared by Fiesta, to families of children with disabilities notifying them of scheduled training dates/times and topics. Flyers were mailed and phone blasts conducted prior to each training session. Fiesta Educativa employees (and in some cases, parent volunteers from individual school sites) made personal phone calls to families prior to each session inviting them to attend. One school raffled off prizes to parents and encouraged students to remind their parents by offering homework passes or other student-specific incentives. Targeting families of children with disabilities is necessary in order to ensure that session content meets their specific needs and experiences. All presentations and materials were provided in Spanish. The agency also provided participants with binders to organize training materials.

EVIDENCE OF SUCCESS

To evaluate the effectiveness of Fiesta Educativa's work with families, an external evaluation team obtained information and feedback through archival data (e.g., flyers, PowerPoint presentations, handouts, sign-in sheets, and session evaluations), parent surveys, and semistructured interviews with participating parents and site administrators. Parent participants completed brief surveys during the first and final sessions of the training series. The survey (in both Spanish and English) included 16 items addressing major content areas of the training curriculum, such as indicating how much they agreed or disagreed with a series of statements. After completing the training program, 38 parents who attended at least three sessions were asked to participate in semistructured phone interviews lasting between 15 and 30 minutes with a trained bilingual interviewer. Phone interviews allowed the evaluation team to obtain more in-depth information regarding parents' participation and survey item responses. During phone interviews, parent participants were asked a series of open-ended questions regarding the effectiveness of program goals. Administrators from each site were also interviewed in person at the end of the training sessions at their site regarding benefits and obstacles related to the program's implementation.

Survey and posttraining interview data suggested that over 80% of the parents reported high levels of self-efficacy regarding their knowledge of and ability to communicate with their child's school, support their child's special education program, support their child's social skills and behavior at home, and access community resources for their child with disabilities. Overall, parents reported learning important information related to school programming, home support, and community resources in a manner that was responsive to families' linguistic, cultural, and personal needs. The benefits of collaboration between a community agency and schools are clear. Through this program, schools were able to provide their CLD families of children with disabilities with training and support in their primary language.

Future Plans of FE

Fiesta Educativa would like to partner with other school districts to obtain additional funding in order to continue this type of work. Collaborating with a district partner from the initial planning stages would benefit the overall program while meeting the needs of parents, their children with disabilities, schools, teachers, and other important stakeholders. As an organization, Fiesta Educativa will continue to develop its capacity to become a community partner in research and raise consciousness among families regarding the importance of research. Other programs to develop or in development include the Autism Parent Education Program, the Trainers-of-Trainers parent leadership program, and the Transition and Employment Services for Young Adults with Disabilities program.

LEARNING RIGHTS LAW CENTER

Community Organization and Program Background

The second community organization that offers support to families of children with disabilities is the Learning Rights Law Center (LRLC). Located in southern California since it was founded in 2005, the LRLC is an independent nonprofit organization offering legal training, education, and services. Its mission is to ensure that all students have equitable access to the public education system, with a focus on students with learning difficulties. The LRLC believes that grassroots legal advocacy can improve the public education system and that parents should be equal partners in the advocacy process. As a result, the LRLC established TIGER (Training Individuals for Grassroots Education Reform) as a method for providing special education advocacy training for families in need.

TIGER uses a multidisciplinary approach in working with other organizations to educate parents regarding the education rights of their children with disabilities. Since parents are the best advocates for their children, TIGER prioritizes addressing the most urgent and unmet needs of families via self-advocacy. These include understanding their children's basic special education rights, understanding special education procedural safeguards, and advocating in IEP meetings with school district representatives. In collaboration with Loyola Marymount University and Kaiser Permanente's Watts Counseling and Learning Center, the TIGER program works directly with low-income minority families, including a high number of Spanish-speaking families in Los Angeles County's highest poverty areas. From 2005 to 2012, more than 1,200 individuals have participated. The following section describes the components and promising practices of an effective training program in special education advocacy for CLD families.

Program Components for Special Education Advocacy

TIGER Training Cohorts

The LRLC organized the *Beginners TIGER* cohort in collaboration with Kaiser Permanente's Watts Counseling Center. The Watts *Beginners TIGER* group provides co-facilitated training sessions in Spanish and English by attorneys and staff at the Watts Center for groups of 15 to 40 parents per session. The group meets monthly for approximately 4 hours on Saturdays. Childcare is provided at the center while parents attend training. Parents must apply to participate in the beginners group and commit to attending the monthly training for a year. In 2011, the LRLC organized a similar beginners group in East Los Angeles (East LA *Beginners TIGER*) specifically targeted for parents with children, 3 through 7 years of age, with disabilities.

During *Beginners TIGER* sessions, parents organize, review, and reference their child's IEPs and educational documents, including school evaluation reports, letters, report cards, meeting notifications, and progress reports. Facilitators cover major components of special education content knowledge including annual goals, assessment, and accommodations. Following these presentations, parents engage in hands-on activities requiring them to practice a particular skill covered during the session (e.g., letter writing, identify goals, measuring progress). Time is allocated in each session for parents to ask general questions related to the session topic. Families are encouraged to problem solve during these question-and-answer exchanges, apply what they have learned, and support one another. This discussion format allows parents to increase their participation and confidence in a supportive environment.

The *Advanced TIGER* cohort includes parents who have already completed the *Beginners TIGER* training. Monthly training, conducted in English and Spanish, is organized around major topic areas addressed in the curriculum. Training topics include compliance complaints, transition services, independent evaluations, and IEP implementation. These topics are determined based on the needs shared by participants from the various cohorts. Advanced training includes lecture presentations led by LRLC attorneys along with staff from Loyola Marymount University and Kaiser's Watts Center.

Parent Curriculum

Parent training focuses on reviewing essential content from the *Special Education Toolkit* and strategies to facilitate parent advocacy. A major foundation for trainings across TIGER cohorts is the development and use of the *Special Education Toolkit*. The Toolkit is a self-advocacy guide developed by the LRLC for parents and facilitators and is provided in both English and Spanish. See Table 7.1 for an outline of topic areas addressed in the Toolkit curriculum. The LRLC staff and attorneys continually update the Toolkit for accuracy and accessibility to parents and facilitators.

In addition to the essential Toolkit content, TIGER trainers use training sessions to cover essential special education advocacy skills with parents. One of the first skills parents learn to master is the organization of their child's records that are related to his/her special education program and services. Parents learn not only which documents are important but also understand the information these documents contain (e.g., services, goals, present levels of performance). Trainers encourage parents to refer to their

Table 7.1.   Special Education Toolkit

• Introduction	• Placement & Least Restrictive Environment
• Statistics	
• Relevant Laws and Cases	• Enrollment and Interim Placement
• Navigating the Special Education System	• Transition Services
• Child Find	• Behavior Issues and Discipline
• Eligibility	• Mental Health
• Assessments and Reassessments	• Parents/Surrogate Rights
• Records	• Early Childhood
• Individualized Program Plan & Triennial	• Delinquent and Dependent Youth
• Free Appropriate Public Education	• Disputes and Stay-Put
• Goals	• Sample Letters
• Related/Supplemental Services	• Accommodations & Modifications

binders and documents during training in order to apply what they learn to their child's special education programming. Trainers also assist parents in understanding how best to prepare for and participate during IEP meetings, such as reviewing the last IEP to become more familiar with the previous goals and levels of performance, as well as the services (frequency, location, duration) identified to support areas of need.

Lastly, home-school communication is an essential skill TIGER trainers address with families. LRLC trainers encourage parents to communicate regularly with their child's teacher. Letter writing is an essential skill all parents should master. Letters allow school staff to keep track of parents' requests or concerns. Parents should communicate in the language they feel most comfortable using.

Community Groups

After attending TIGER training for many years, several long-term TIGER parent participants, "parent leaders," began to organize monthly support groups in their respective communities. As of now, there are three parent groups, which consist of families with children from schools within the same local community and having a variety of disabilities. TIGER parent leaders continue to receive support from the LRLC staff and partners (Kaiser's Watts Center and LMU). Types of support include assisting parent leaders with troubleshooting issues related to the implementation of their community groups such as obtaining necessary bilingual resources and supporting parents at different levels of knowledge regarding special education. Monthly community group meetings are held in homes or community centers and are entirely planned, implemented, and supported by the parent leaders themselves. These gatherings allow parents to share with one another their struggles and accomplishments related to supporting their child with a disability. During meeting, parents also share information regarding school (e.g., navigating IEPs, special services) and community resources (e.g., regional centers, local trainings, free clinics). Overall, the community groups are built on a grassroots, parents-supporting-parents model.

Townhall

Given the TIGER Program's widespread interest, the LRLC organized its first annual TIGER Townhall in 2010, inviting participants and community groups to gather at Loyola Marymount University. The purpose of the TIGER Townhall is to allow parents from a variety of communities to discuss common areas of concern and develop action plans to support these needs. In 2012, the annual TIGER Townhall included morning training sessions in areas previously identified by communities, and afternoon community group meetings to create year-long action plans to address common concerns. See Table 7.2 for an example of a facilitator's guide developed by the LRLC for community group meetings during Townhall. Facilitators from Learning Rights and its partners assist community groups to prepare for this work before, during, and after the Townhall.

EVIDENCE OF SUCCESS

In 2012, parent participants in the *Beginning TIGER* cohort completed a pre- and postsurvey regarding their knowledge of a variety of skills necessary to support their child's programming. These included being able to understand their legal rights, organize their records, prepare for IEP meetings, and monitor their child's progress. Surveys were administered at the beginning and end of the program and completed by parents in either Spanish or English, according to parents' language preference. Survey results indicated that 28 families who participated in one of two *Beginning TIGER* cohort groups reported gains in multiple skill areas by program completion, such as understanding how to write a letter to the school regarding their child, ask for changes in their child's IEP, and request for evaluations.

In addition to parent participants, community parent leaders ($n =$ 15) completed surveys in either Spanish or English to determine their satisfaction with their ability to support themselves and other families and to describe the issues experienced by parents within their community group. These parent leaders expressed feeling more confident with their

**Table 7.2.   Townhall Facilitator Guide
(Modified Townhall Facilitator's Form,
Learning Rights Law Center, 2012).**

COMMUNITY GROUP PRETOWNHALL PREPARATION

Issue Selected & Rationale:_____

1. Is this an ongoing problem?
2. Explain the effect this issue has on families in your community.
3. Propose 3 practical solutions to your problem.
4, How did your group come to select this issue?

TOWNHALL FACILITATION INSTRUCTIONS

1. *Introductions & Ground Rules:* Have parents introduce themselves.

2. *Review Task:* Review the group's selected issue and the purpose for today's work.

   • Develop 1 to 3 long-term objectives to address community group issue.

   • Develop concrete steps to address long-term objectives. Include at minimum:

   –Action required   –Necessary resources
   –Necessary activities   –Methods to monitor progress toward
   –Timeline & contacts   specified outcome

3. *Develop Objectives:* Develop 1 to 2 long-term objectives to address issue.

4. *Develop Action Plan:*

   • Complete planning grid. (feel free to fill out on larger paper/or on laptop.)

   • Action Planning considerations to keep in mind:

   –Be action oriented   –Consider necessary resources
   –Set realistic timelines   –Determine how to monitor progress

knowledge and skills and sharing this information with other parents. They also reported observing their families feeling more independent during IEPs, understanding how to communicate through letter writing, and obtaining more services for their children. Overall, according to parent leaders, community group families have expressed gratitude to the LRLC and TIGER parent leaders for their ongoing support.

Future Plans for TIGER

The Learning Rights Law Center will continue to further its vision and invest its resources on the implementation and continued growth of the TIGER program. The organization plans to expand much-needed Beginner cohort training into communities in southern California, such as the Inland Empire. An increasing parent interest in the community groups has motivated the LRLC to collaborate with these groups more strategically and identify the LRLC's role in supporting their work. Learning Rights is in the process of developing a Parent Advisory Board to assist with ongoing decisions related to TIGER's programing; areas of emphasis for local-, regional-, and state-level activities; and topics for training. The organization is in the process of formalizing its teaching materials and curriculum with an eye toward replicating the program.

CONCLUSION

After describing the work of both of these nonprofit community agencies and the promising practices they have shared with parents and schools, it is clear that CLD parents can gain access to essential information to make a difference in the life of their child with disabilities. Engaging in collaborative relationships with community agencies able to supply needed resources can support schools and families toward building parents' capital resources and in turn strengthening their ability to participate in their child's special education programming.

Reflecting back to the parent's statement at the beginning of this chapter, we find that diverse families new to the United States and unfamiliar with the educational system quickly realize the incredible obstacles they face in their journey to support their child with disabilities. The desire to change this unfortunate landscape is expressed so clearly by this Learning Rights TIGER parent leader:

> *Hay muchas necesidades en mi comunidad, en habla hispana (población hispana), que venimos de otros países adaptándonos a una nueva vida, a un sistema diferente y que lamentablemente no tuvimos oportunidades de educación como los nacidos o creídos aquí. Hay muchos obstáculos por vencer, mucho por hacer. Quiero ser parte de este cambio.*

(There are many needs in my community, in Spanish speaking, Hispanic populations, that we come from other countries adapting to a new life, to a different system and unfortunately we did not have educational opportunities like those born or raised here. There are many obstacles to defeat, a lot to do. I want to be part of this change.)

Through the collaborative efforts of schools and community agencies, CLD parents, like this parent leader, can become better equipped to participate in the educational process and more confidently support their child with disabilities.

AUTHOR'S NOTE

For more information regarding the organizations discussed in this chapter, *Fiesta Educativa*, and the *Learning Rights Law Center*, please refer to their respective websites: http://www.fiestaeducativa.org, http://www.learningrights.org.

REFERENCES

Blanchette, W. J., Klingner, J. K., & Harry, B. (2009). The intersection of race, culture, language, and disability. *Urban Education, 44*(4), 389–409.

Bourdieu, P. (1986). The forms of capital. In J. G. Richardson (Ed.), *Handbook of theory and research for the sociology of education* (pp. 241–258). New York, NY: Greenwood.

Bronfenbrenner, U. (1986). Ecology of the family as a context for human development: Research perspectives. *Developmental Psychology, 22*(6), 723–742.

Erwin, E. J., & Soodak, L. C. (2008). The evolving relationship between families of children with disabilities and professionals. In T. C. Jimenez & V. L. Graf (Eds.), *Education for all: Critical issues in the education of children and youth with disabilities* (pp. 35–69). San Francisco, CA: Jossey-Bass.

Fiesta Educativa, Inc. (2007). [Home page.] Retrieved December 15, 2012, from http://www.fiestaeducativa.org/home.html

Gomez Mandac, C., Rudd, R., Hehir, T., & Acevedo-Garcia, D. (2012). Readability of special education procedural safeguards. *The Journal of Special Education, 45*(4), 195–203.

Harry, B. (2008). Collaboration with culturally and linguistically diverse families: Ideal versus reality. *Exceptional Children, 74*, 372–388.

Harry, B., & Klingner, J. K. (2006). *Why are so many minority students in special education? Understanding race and disability in schools.* New York, NY: Teachers College Press.

Langdon, H. W. (2009). Providing optimal special education services to Hispanic children and their families. *Communication Disorders Quarterly, 30*(2), 83–96.

Lo, L. (2009). Collaborating with Chinese families of children with hearing impairments. *Communication Disorders Quarterly, 30*(2), 97–102.

Shapiro, J., Monzó, L. D., Rueda, R., Gomez, J. A., & Blacher, J. (2004). Alienated advocacy: Perspectives of Latina mothers of young adults with developmental disabilities on service systems. *Mental Retardation, 42*(1), 37–54.

Tejero-Hughes, M., Valle-Riestra, D. M., & Arguelles, M. E. (2008). The voices of Latino families raising children with special needs. *Journal of Latinos and Education, 7*(3), 241–257.

Trainor, A. A. (2010). Diverse approaches to parent advocacy during special education home-school interactions. *Remedial and Special Education, 31*(1), 34–47.

Turnbull, A., Turnbull, R., Erwin, E. J., Soodak, L. C., & Shogren, K. A. (2011). *Families, professionals and exceptionality: Positive outcomes through partnerships and trust* (6th ed.). Upper Saddle River, NJ: Pearson Education.

Weiss, H. B., & Lopez, M. E. (2010). Community support for family engagement in children's learning. In H. B. Weiss, H. Kreider, M. E. Lopez, & C. Chatt-man-Nelson (Eds.), *Preparing educators to engage families: Case studies using an ecological systems framework* (pp. 32–27). Thousand Oaks, CA: Sage.

Zoints, L. T., Zoints, P., Harrison, S., & Bellinger, O. (2003). Urban African Ameri-can families' perceptions of cultural sensitivity within the special education system. *Focus on Autism and Other Developmental Disabilities, 18,* 41–50.

PART III

PRACTICES IN ASIAN COUNTRIES

CHAPTER 8

A SCHOOL-BASED PARENT SUPPORT GROUP

Empowering Hong Kong Parents of Children With Disabilities to be Advocates

Lusa Lo, Tak-foo Cheng, and Kwok-Ching Chan

INTRODUCTION

As the principle of including all students with diverse needs and providing them with equal opportunities to learn emerged decades ago, inclusive education has become a global movement of education reform in many countries. Similar to many parts in the world, the importance of providing services that cater to the individualized needs of students with disabilities and enabling them to be exposed to the same curriculum as their peers without disabilities is strongly emphasized in the Hong Kong (HK) schools (Lian, 2008; Lian, Tse, & Li , 2007). Due to the structure of the educational system in HK, parents are under immense pressure to make sure that their children with disabilities are making appropriate progress in

Promising Practices to Empower Culturally and Linguistically Diverse Families of Children With Disabilities, pp. 113–124

their inclusion classes. Additionally, these parents are in need of information regarding how to assist their children academically at home. However, support for these parents is often limited.

BRIEF HISTORY OF
HONG KONG SPECIAL EDUCATION SYSTEM

The first self-contained special education school for the deaf was established in 1935 (Board of Education, 1996). Gradually, more special education schools were created to serve children with various types of disabilities, such as visual impairment, physical impairment, and intellectual disabilities. Beginning in the late 1990s, the HK government emphasized the importance of allowing all children to have equal opportunities to achieve to their maximum potential and called for schools to implement inclusive education through the adoption of Whole School Approaches (Education Bureau, 2008). Since then, the number of students with disabilities has increased dramatically in regular schools. In the last six years, there was an increase of 116% elementary students with disabilities and 400% secondary students with disabilities in regular schools (Education Bureau, 2012a). Their disabilities included specific learning disabilities, intellectual disability, autism spectrum disorders, attention deficit/hyperactivity disorder, physical disability, visual impairment, hearing impairment, and speech and language impairment.

At the initial stage of the implementation of inclusive education, due to the lack of resources and special education training of general education teachers, many HK schools were reluctant to support the movement (Michael, 2004; Poon-McBrayer, 2005). The Education Bureau, researchers, and practitioners worked collaboratively and determined ways to support schools, teachers, parents, and children with disabilities. First, schools were allowed to use the allocated funds to provide support to teachers and students with disabilties. Schools could also apply for grants from the Education Bureau, allowing them to "buy" additional services from nonprofit organizations, catering to the needs of students with disabilities. These services included, but were not limited to, speech therapy, educational psychology service, and learning support (Education Bureau, 2011).

Second, the Education Bureau formulated a 5-year teacher professional development framework, which provided teachers of elementary, secondary, and special schools with basic, advanced, and thematic courses that enhanced their abilities to serve and support students with disabilities in the inclusion classrooms (Education Bureau, 2007). By the end of the 5-year period, each school was expected to have a certain percentage of teachers complete the courses in each of the three levels. Recently, the

Education Bureau has extended this plan, so more schools could achieve the goals that were set in the framework (Education Bureau, 2012b).

Finally, the importance of family and school partnerships was greatly emphasized (Board of Education, 1996). Research consistently suggested that children performed more successfully when parents were highly engaged in their children's academic career (Henderson & Mapp, 2002; Ingersoll & Dvortcsak, 2006; Jeynes, 2007). HK schools were encouraged to utilize various ways to actively involve parents so they would know how to support their children at home and help them make appropriate progress.

HK has a very competitive educational system. Many parents are eager to enroll their children in prestigious schools. They believe that by doing so, their children are more likely to receive the best education, get into colleges and/or universities, and work in high-paying jobs. Although the Education Bureau has implemented a new school placement system that attempts to eliminate the pressure that may have been imposed on young children by the intense competition to enter prestigious schools (Education Bureau, 2010), test scores are still heavily used to determine a student's learning ability. HK students are being tested several times a year. The average of a student's 5th- and 6th-grade test results is used to determine his/her secondary school placement. Students with mild to moderate disabilities who happen to have high test scores and are able to enter a prestigious secondary school are under immense pressure to maintain their grades. However, as schoolwork gets more demanding and requires more group work, secondary students with disabilities who lack organizational and social skills are less likely to succeed in schools (Bryan, Burstein, & Bryan, 2001; Milsom, 2007). Parents of these children with disabilities often do not know how to support them at home. They are in need of resources and support.

BENEFITS OF PARENT SUPPORT GROUPS

Discovering that your child has a disability can be devastating for many families. Parents of children with disabilities go through a cycle of mixed feelings about their child's diagnosis, such as denial, anger, grief, fear, guilt, confusion, powerlessness, disappointment, and rejection (National Information Center for Children and Youth with Disabilities, 2003; Sheehey & Sheehey, 2007). Many families of children with disabilities feel that they may not have the ability to change the outcomes of their child's disability (Twoy, Connolly, & Novak, 2008). For families who are from diverse cultures, accepting that they have a child with a disability is even more difficult, since their cultural views of disability are often different from those who are from the dominant culture (Lamorey, 2002; Lo, 2009). Many of these families believe that the causes of their child's disability are sins committed by their parents or their ancestors or are due to certain kinds of food intake during the pregnancy (Chan & Chen, 2011). With these cultural beliefs, they not only need information and resources regarding their children's disability and how to advocate for their children, but also psychological and emotional support.

Twoy and his colleages (2008) examined the coping strategies that were used by 55 parents of children with disabilities. They found that 93% of the parent participants sought information and advice from other families who had faced similar problems, while 80% of them sought support from community agencies and programs. In another related study, Solomon, Pistrang, and Barker (2001) examined the perception of 56 parents of children with disabilities regarding the helpfulness of participating in support groups. These parents reported that by participating in the support groups, they were able to gain knowledge and skills that prepared them for coping with their child's disabilities and improving their parenting skills. Similar results were found in Lo's (2010) study that, due to cultural and language challenges, these families were eager to meet other Chinese families of children with disabilities who had gone through similar challenges. Lo examined the reasons and investigated the perceive benefits of 15 Chinese parents of children with disabilities who participated in support groups. They reported that their participation in the support group gave them a sense of belonging. They were empowered to handle issues regarding their children with disabilities. Findings of these studies indicated that having access to a support network was beneficial to families of children with disabilities. They not only gained information to improve their ways of working with their children with disabilities and skills to advocate for their children, but also obtained emotional support from their fellow parent members in the groups (Banach, Iudice, Conway, & Couse, 2010; Drake, Couse, DiNapoli, & Banach, 2008).

Parent support groups can be initiated and organized by various parties. Most of them are organized by parents of children with disabilities or community organizations. Some support groups serve families of children with various disabilities, while others only serve families of children with a particular type of disability, such as autism spectrum disorders, attention deficit/hyperactivity disorder, or Down syndrome (Family Ties of Massachusetts, 2012). Regardless of the types of support groups, their mission is to provide support to families of children with disabilities.

While all the studies focus on the effectiveness of community-based parent support groups, none of them examines the impact of school-based support groups on parents of children with disabilities. Since schools and parents may have difficulty agreeing on which services and how much services would be suitable for the student with disabilities, instead of turning to schools for support, parents prefer seeking assistance through community organizations. Furthermore, in the Chinese culture, school professionals are often considered as authority figures (Chan & Chen, 2011). Parents rarely seek support from schools. When parents are invited to schools, it is usually about some concerns schools have about their children. In other words, schools and parents remain in the active-passive roles. Parents rarely view themselves as schools' partners. However, one secondary school in HK values the importance of empowering and supporting the families they serve. A school staff collaborated with a parent of a child with disabilities and organized a school-based support group. The purpose of this chapter is to discuss the impact of this group on empowering parents of children with disabilities to be their child's advocates and school partners.

PROMISING PRACTICES

Background Information of School

This study was conducted at the CNEC Lau Wing Sang Secondary School, which was established in 1999. This secondary school, of Christian background, was located in a district that was populated mainly by families of low socioeconomic status. Students' ages ranged from 12 to 19. In 2011–2012, the school had approximately 1,200 students. About 4% of the students had a diagnosed disability, which was an increase of 200% in students with disabilities since 2006. Their disabilities included specific learning disabilities, autism spectrum disorders, attention deficit/hyperactivity disorder, physical disability, visual impairment, hearing impairment, and speech and language impairment.

To address the philosophy of the Whole School Approach in integrated education, various types of professional development training were offered to teachers. The goals were to cultivate an inclusive school culture and enable teachers to learn about the different types of disabilities and understand the rationale of integrated education. All students with disabilities in the school were supported by various teams of staff who had extensive background in special education, such as the counseling team and integrated education team, which was composed of teachers and student guidance counselors.

Formation of School-Based Parent Support Group

Due to the rapid increase in students with disabilities in the school, the integrated education team was interested in determining ways to support parents of children with disabilities. After speaking with many teachers and parents in the school, a parent of a child with Asperger's disorder and attention deficit/hyperactivity disorder and one of the student guidance counselors felt that there was a need to form a school-based parent support group. The main goal of the group was to enable parents of children with disabilities to meet other parents who had a child with similar disabilities and obtain and share supports and resources.

After consulting with the principal and teachers, the student guidance officer identified and contacted 10 parents who could benefit from participating in the support group. Due to work schedule and/or family responsibilities, only five parents attended the first meeting, which took place in one of the school's conference rooms in September 2008. Their child's disabilities were autism spectrum disorders and attention deficit/hyperactivity disorders. Since then, the number of parents attending the monthly meetings increased from 5 to 14 parents. See Table 8.1 for the demographics of the parent participants.

The student guidance officer and a teacher who is an integrated education team member coordinated this school-based support group. The group meets once a month, on the second Monday of each month, from 7 to 9 P.M., in one of the conference rooms or the auditorium at the school. Parent volunteers take turns bringing food to share with the group. Some parents choose to order take-out food, while others bring homemade food. The first 30 minutes of each meeting is designated for dinner and networking. The school principal always drops by the meeting during this time to greet parents. Once the official group meeting begins, the principal leaves the meeting. This ensures that parents feel comfortable sharing their concerns with the group. All discussions in the monthly meeting are kept confidential. Per parents' requests, some discussions or concerns will be shared with the principal.

The parents determine all meeting topics. At the end of each school year, the group meets and discusses the meeting topics for the upcoming year. In the last 5 years, the meeting topics included

1. Various trainings offered by guest speakers from nonprofit organizations, specialists, and university faculty members. Topics included, but were not limited to, managing time, parenting skills, handling stress, and addressing students' puberty issues.
2. Gospel messages sharing.
3. Off-campus activities, such as visiting members' home and supporting members at their baptism ceremonies.
4. Recreational activities, such as learning relaxation exercises, dancing, and making lip balms.

Table 8.1. Demographics of the Parent Participants

Demographics	Number of Participants
Age	
30–40	3
40–50	8
50–60	3
Education	
Elementary	1
Elementary graduates	1
High school	1
High school graduates	1
Associate degree or diploma	8
Master's degree	1
Number of Years Participated in This Support Group	
< 1 year	2
1–2 years	5
3–4 years	7
Their Child's Disabilities	
Autism spectrum disorders	7
Emotional and behavioral disorder	2
Attention deficit/hyperactivity disorder	7
Their Child's Grade	
Form 1 (equivalent to 7th grade)	1
Form 2 (equivalent to 8th grade)	4
Form 3 (equivalent to 9th grade)	2
Form 4 (equivalent to 10th grade)	4
Form 5 (equivalent to 11th grade)	1
Form 6 (equivalent to 12th grade)	1
Graduated	1

OUTCOMES

In order to determine the effectiveness of the support group, a parent survey of 21 questions was given to the parent participants. The survey consisted of 14 Likert-scale questions ranging from 1 to 4 (1 = strongly disagree; 4 = strongly agree) and 7 open-ended questions (see Table 8.2 for sample questions). The open-ended questions were used to validate parent responses in the Likert-scale questions and determine how the parent support group could be improved.

Table 8.2.   Sample Survey Questions

Types of Questions	Sample Questions
Likert-scale	1. Since I participated in this support group, I am able to obtain useful information to support my child with a disability at home.
	2. After participating in this support group, I feel that I am taking an active role to help make this school better.
Open-ended	1. Please indicate three previous meeting topics that were most helpful to you.
	2. What suggestions would you like to offer to the group coordinators so the functions and organizations of this group can be improved and/or expanded?

Parent Perceptions of the Support Group

The survey results indicated the following:

1. Parents were satisfied with the organization and structure of the group ($M = 3.4$).
2. All parents strongly agreed ($n = 8$) or agreed ($n = 6$) that other parents of children with disabilities should participate in this support group.
3. Among the 14 parent participants, the main reason they participated in the support group was to obtain emotional support ($n = 13$), meet other parents of children with disabilities ($n = 12$), obtain information and resources ($n = 12$), and help other parents of children with disabilities ($n = 8$). One parent also indicated that one of her reasons for participating in the group was to expand her social life and relieve stress.
4. All the parents strongly agreed ($n = 9$) or agreed ($n = 5$) that they enjoyed being part of the support group. The parents not only could obtain useful information and resources to support their children with disabilities but also could support other parents of children with disabilities who were in need.
5. Among the parent participants, six of them indicated that, besides the monthly group meetings, they remained in close contact with

other group members. Some of them would connect via phone, share information they learned in other settings, and meet for other activities, such as hiking and going out for dinner.

6. Some parents felt that their active participation in the group empowered them to take an active role in the school and improve the organization of the school ($M = 3.2$).

Recommendations to Group Coordinators

In addition to evaluating the parent perceptions of the support group, parents were asked to offer suggestions to the group coordinators so the functions of the group could be improved.

1. *Recruiting more new parents and sharing more.* Parent participants felt that it was important for them to learn from other parents of children with disabilities, such as handling their children's behavioral issues. The parents suggested the role of coordinators to connect with classroom teachers and identify the students who were in need, so more parents of children with disabilities could participate in the group. In addition, although having guest speakers was helpful, parents felt that they wanted more opportunities to share their experiences and concerns.

2. *Use parents' concern to organize meetings.* A few parents suggested that the group coordinators could solicit parents' concerns and use them to structure each monthly group meeting. Additionally, meeting topics should be established early so parents could plan accordingly.

3. *Balance meeting topics.* Although parent participants continue to be interested in learning more about issues that were related to their child's disability, they felt that the group coordinators could also organize some outdoor activities, such as going out for barbecue or having festive gatherings. This would allow the parents to spend more time with fellow members.

4. *Obtain more support from the parent participants.* The parents indicated that, in addition to participating in the group, they were interested in contributing more so the group coordinators' workload could be reduced. They suggested that the group coordinators could assign two parents at a time to help preparing for each monthly meeting, such as contacting and reminding parents to attend.

FUTURE PLANS AND CONCLUSIONS

The evidence supports that the parent participants are pleased with the current school-based support group. They not only can receive information and resources, but also develop friendships with other families who face similar challenges. In the upcoming year, besides addressing the suggestions that were made by the participants, the school is interested in empowering a few of the current members to be parent leaders. The survey data suggested that several parents are eager to support other parents of children with disabilities but may lack confidence. The school plans to organize parent leader training for those who are interested in supporting other parents of children with disabilities. Furthermore, the group coordinator plans to have frequent meetings with classroom teachers and determine if any students with disabilities and their parents are in need of support. She can then invite these parents to attend some recreational activities that are organized by the support group. These opportunities will enable them to meet the parents in the group and learn more about how the group functions. When these new parents feel comfortable, they may be more likely to be part of the support group.

Having children with disabilities can be a difficult journey for many parents. Schools have the responsibility to guide and support these families. In addition to providing families with information, creating a comfortable environment for parents to share, network, and receive emotional and psychological support is crucial. Schools should also utilize creative ways to explore resources, such as partnering with community organizations, to support families. The ones who benefit from this partnership are our students with disabilities.

REFERENCES

Banach, M., Iudice, J., Conway, L., & Couse, L. (2010). Family support and empowerment: Post autism diagnosis support group for parents. *Social Work with Groups, 33,* 69–83.

Board of Education. (1996). *Report of the sub-committee on special education.* Hong Kong, China: Author.

Bryan, T., Burstein, K., & Bryan, J. (2001). Students with learning disabilities: Homework problems and promising practices. *Educational Psychologist, 36,* 167–180.

Chan, S., & Chen, D. (2011). Families with Asian roots. In E. Lynch & M. Hanson (Eds.), *Developing cross-cultural competence: A guide for working with children and their families* (4th ed., pp. 219–298). Baltimore, MD: Paul H. Brookes.

Drake, J., Couse, L., DiNapoli, P., & Banach, M. (2008). Interdisciplinary best practice: A case study of family and school support for a young child with

ASD. *International Journal of Nursing in Intellectual and Development Disabilities, 4*, article 3.

Education Bureau. (2007). *Teacher professional development framework on integrated education (Education Bureau Circular No. 13/2007)*. Hong Kong, China: Author.

Education Bureau. (2008). *Operation guide on the whole school approach to integrated education*. Hong Kong, China: Author.

Education Bureau. (2010). *Kindergarten, primary and secondary education: School places allocation systems*. Retrieved from http://www.edb.gov.hk/index.aspx?nodeID=1496&langno=1

Education Bureau. (2011). *Special education*. Hong Kong, China: Author.

Education Bureau. (2012a). *Press releases and publications: Special education*. Retrieved from http://www.edb.gov.hk/index.aspx?nodeID=1040&langno=1

Education Bureau. (2012b). *Teacher professional development on catering for students with special educational needs (SEN)*. Retrieved from http://www.edb.gov.hk/en/edu-system/special/sen-training/index.html

Family Ties of Massachusetts. (2012). *Support groups*. Retrieved from http://mass-familyties.org/info/groups.php

Henderson, A., & Mapp, K. (2002). *A new wave of evidence: The impact of school, family, and community connections on student achievement*. Austin, TX: Southwest Educational Development Laboratory.

Ingersoll, B., & Dvortcsak, A. (2006). Including parent training in the early childhood special education curriculum for children with autism spectrum disorders. *Topics in Early Childhood Special Education, 26*, 179–187.

Jeynes, W. H. (2007). The relationship between parental involvement and urban secondary school student academic achievement: A meta-analysis. *Urban Education, 42*, 82–109.

Lamorey, S. (2002). The effects of culture on special education services: Evil eyes, prayer meetings, and IEPs. *Teaching Exceptional Children, 34*, 67–71.

Lian, M.-G. (2008, December). *Backgrounds and efforts in enhancing inclusive education in Hong Kong, Taiwan, and the United States*. Paper presented at the Special and Inclusive Education Seminar, Taipei Municipal Unversity of Education, Taipei, Taiwan.

Lian, M.-G., Tse, C.-Y., & Li, A. (2007). Special education in Hong Kong: Background, contemporary trends and issues in programs for learners with disabilities. *The Journal of International Association of Special Education, 8*, 5–19.

Lo, L. (2009). Collaborating with Chinese families of children with hearing impairments. *Communication Disorders Quarterly, 30*, 97–102.

Lo, L. (2010). Perceived benefits experienced in support groups for Chinese families of children with disabilities. *Early Child Development and Care, 180*(3), 405–415.

Michael, R. (2004). *Let's talk integration!* Paper presented at the Hong Kong Red Cross 50th anniversary Special Education and Rehabilitation Services Conference, Hong Kong, China.

Milsom, A. (2007). Interventions to assist students with disabilities through school transitions. *Professional School Counseling, 10*, 1096–2409.

National Information Center for Children and Youth with Disabilities. (2003). *Parenting a child with special needs*. Washington, DC: Author.

Poon-McBrayer, K. (2005). Full inclusion for children with severe learning difficulties: Ideology and reality. *Journal of Interrnational Special Needs Education, 8,* 19–26.

Sheehey, P. H., & Sheehey, P. E. (2007). Elements for successful parent-professional collaboration: The fundamental things apply as time goes by. *Teaching Exceptional Children Plus, 4,* article 3. Retrieved from http://escholarship.bc.edu/education/tecplus/vol4/iss2/art3

Solomon, M., Pistrang, N., & Barker, C. (2001). The benefits of mutual support groups for parents of children with disabilities. *American Journal of Community Psychology, 29,* 113–132.

Twoy, R., Connolly, P., & Novak, J. (2008). Coping strategies used by parents of children with autism. *Journal of the American Academy of Nurse Practitioners, 19,* 251–260.

CHAPTER 9

PARENT ADVOCACY GROUPS IN TAIWAN

Support for Families of Children With Disabilities

Hsiu-Zu Ho, Min Chia Tang, Whitney J. Detar, and Mian Wang

CULTURAL BACKGROUND

Each culture's customs and beliefs shape the worldviews and behaviors in that particular society. Lamorey (2002, p. 67) stated, "Each culture has its own explanations for why some babies are born with disabilities, how these children are to be treated, and what responsibilities and roles are expected of family members, helpers, and other members of the society." In Taiwan, the social attitudes toward children with disabilities are indeed strongly influenced by cultural values and beliefs. For example, Confucianism, Buddhism, and collectivistic traditions all have a great impact on Taiwanese culture, including societal perspectives on disability. Based on the Confucian concept of the preservation of harmony, Taiwanese family members are typically reluctant to share unpleasant news or information that does

Promising Practices to Empower Culturally and Linguistically Diverse Families of Children With Disabilities, pp. 125–142
Copyright © 2014 by Information Age Publishing

125

not follow the social norm. Accordingly, Taiwanese families of children with disabilities are less apt to share their experiences and needs with persons outside of the family circle; and they typically feel they have the primary, if not sole, responsibility of taking care of their own. Influenced by Buddhism, a traditional belief held by some Taiwanese families is that a child's disability is karmic punishment from past moral violations (Chang & McConkey, 2008). This belief may, in part, serve to promote societal stigma toward disability, and consequently, many parents of children with disabilities are less willing to seek support and participate in social activities, hence further isolating themselves from society (Zhou, 2000). Parent advocacy groups have played an important role in providing families with the support they need as well as in impacting public opinion and public policy (Azzopardi, 2000; Black & Baker, 2011).

In the disability rights movement, parents have historically served in key advocacy roles. The role of parents as political advocates for the passage of the U.S. special education law, IDEA, is well documented (Turnbull & Turnbull, 1996). Turnbull and Turnbull (2001) define advocacy as "taking one's own or another's perspective to obtain a result not otherwise available" (p. 350). In a qualitative study of over 100 American parents of individuals with disabilities, Wang, Mannan, Turnbull, Poston, and Summers (2004) found parents to perceive advocacy as an obligation and a means to improve services. They also found parent advocacy to enhance parents' coping ability in facing challenges related to their children with disabilities. Though consistency of participation in parent advocacy/support groups varies, some research suggests that parents who do participate tend to perceive higher levels of social support and less isolation than those who do not participate in any groups (Azzopardi, 2000; Black & Baker, 2011; Sadoski, 1999). Studies have found multiple benefits to parents' participation in support/advocacy groups, including increases in parent empowerment surrounding the family, service system, and community (Banach, Iudice, Conway, & Couse, 2010; Solomon, Pistrang, & Barker, 2001), decreases in parent stress (Guralnick, Hammond, Neville, & Connor, 2008), and increases in parents' ability to advocate on behalf of their children (Law, King, Stewart, & King, 2001). Some studies, on the other hand, have revealed advocacy activities to be emotionally draining (Cunconan-Lahr & Brotherson, 1996) and that advocacy involves struggle and can cause stress (Wang et al., 2004). Furthermore, parent advocacy can be greatly influenced by one's cultural values with regard to the expectation for equity, individual rights, and individual/family choice, and this is particularly true of families from culturally and linguistically diverse backgrounds (Kalyanpur, Harry, & Skrtic, 2000).

To provide a fuller context of the status of disabilities in Taiwan and the various types of cultural influences at play, this chapter provides an overview of (a) Taiwan's sociocultural profile; (b) the policies and regulations in

Taiwan on special education as well as those regarding support for families of children with disabilities; and (c) parent advocacy groups in Taiwan that support families of children with disabilities, with particular focus on the practices and successes of the parent advocacy group for Intellectual Disability (ID), namely, the Parents Association for Persons with ID (PAPID). The authors of this chapter utilize an ecocultural theoretical framework connecting ecological contexts, culture, and human behavior (Berry, 1976). The chapter also highlights quotes from a qualitative interview study of parent advocacy group leaders from Taipei, Taiwan. The voices of these advocacy leaders provide insight into Taiwanese parents' perceptions, cultural values and beliefs, experiences, and overall reflections toward family support in Taiwan.

SOCIOCULTURAL PROFILE OF TAIWAN

Demographics

With a population of over 23 million on an island that is approximately 35,000 square kilometers, Taiwan's population density is ranked among the highest in the world (Directorate-General of Budget, Accounting and Statistics, 2011). The people of Taiwan are composed primarily of descendants of the indigenous aborigines (2%) and the Han Chinese (98%), who immigrated to Taiwan from various provinces in China during several historical periods (Directorate-General of Budget, Accounting and Statistics, 2011). The political shifts in the history of Taiwan have played a role in the ethnic identification of the people in Taiwan. While the distinction between "Taiwanese" (typically refers to descendants of early Han immigrants) and "Mainlander" (refers to later Han immigrants who fled along with the Kuomintang in the late 1940s and early 1950s), identities still made today, an increasingly acceptable view is that any individuals with a strong identification with the island's culture can claim to be Taiwanese (Ho, Chen, & Kung, 2008). While Mandarin Chinese is the official language, Taiwanese and Hakka languages are spoken by approximately 70% and 14% of the people in Taiwan, respectively (Ho & Chen, 2013).

Socioeconomic and Political Transformations

During the last several decades, Taiwan successfully transformed from an agrarian labor-intensive economy to a robust capitalistic economy and a leading global market for information and technology in the 21st century. Its rapid economic growth earned it the title of one of the four *Asian*

Tigers (along with Hong Kong, Singapore, and South Korea). Concomitant with these economic changes, Taiwan's political system transformed from authoritarianism (with martial law in effect from 1949 to 1987) to democracy, with its first direct presidential election in 1996. Such transformations have brought changes to a number of traditions, including gender roles and parenting responsibilities (e.g., Ho, Chen, Tran, & Ko, 2010; Ho, Ko, Tran, Phillips, & Chen, 2013; Ho, Yeh, Wu, Tran, & Chen, 2012). These changes have also given rise to a more liberal-minded middle class advocating for rights for underrepresented minority groups with subsequent impact on national policies and educational reforms (Ho & Chen, 2013).

Religious and Cultural Beliefs

Taiwan is diversified in terms of religious faith, with over two dozen registered religions. Buddhism and Taoism are the most common religions, followed by Christianity and other religions (approximately 7%) (CIA, 2013). Except for a small number of temples that are purely Buddhist, most of the island's traditional places of family worship combine Buddhism, Taoism, and folk religions (Ho et al., 2008). Following traditional beliefs, those who believe in reincarnation may view disability as retribution for the amoral behavior of the person with a disability themselves (or of their ancestors) in their previous lives (Chang & McConkey, 2008; Sheng, 1999). These beliefs further stigmatize families of individuals with disabilities, leading to family shame, a sense of inferiority, social rejection, and isolation.

Traditional Chinese customs and superstitions dictate certain practices during pregnancy and after birth, particularly during the first month to ensure a healthy infant. For example, a pregnant woman is to avoid disputes so as to not put a curse on the fetus and disturb its development, avoid using scissors or knives to prevent having a deformed child, and avoid lifting or moving objects in order to prevent miscarriage. During the first month after having a baby, traditional customs and practices regarding the mother's postpartum rest and recovery (termed *zuoyuezi* or *doing the month*) include home rest with avoidance of all household chores, avoidance of washing hair and bathing, eating (e.g., sesame-oil chicken soup), and avoiding certain foods (Chmielowska & Shih, 2007; Pillsbury, 1978). These traditional customs and beliefs tend to place blame on the mother when a child is born with a disability, which means that the child's disability is perceived to be caused, in part, by the mother's lack of adherence to traditional customs and practices during pregnancy and the crucial first month. Given sociocultural changes in Taiwan, one might expect the *zuoyuezi* tradition to fade, yet the custom is still evolving and expanding into contemporary forms and venues, such as the establishment of modern *zuoyuezi* postpartum recovery centers.

Confucian tradition is pervasive in the everyday customs and practices in Taiwanese society and emphasizes moral cultivation of the individual and the harmonious ordering of family and society. Concepts such as collectivistic orientation, social conformity, saving face, respect of elders, filial piety, obligation, submission to authority, and reciprocity-based social relations are rooted in classical Confucian ethics (Ho et al., 2008; Holroyd, 2003). These concepts are also of particular relevance to families of children with disabilities. By traditional expectations, children are to satisfy their parents' wishes, achieve academically, have a successful career, continue the family's ancestral line and ensure the family's future prosperity. Disability, however, is viewed as a condition of disharmony (a threat to social harmony). For example, according to the concept of reciprocity and mutual responsibility, parents have the obligation to take care of their children when they are young, and in turn, children have the obligation to take care of their aging parents. Influenced by this cultural tradition, children born with disabilities have been seen as a dishonor to their families because they are unable to reciprocate and fulfill their obligations in taking care of their elderly parents (Chang & McConkey, 2008).

The Chinese terms used to refer to persons with disabilities are reflective of the traditional cultural beliefs. The traditional terms used are *canfei* and *canji*; the former means "handicap" and "useless"; the latter, "handicap" and "illness" (Liu, 2001). Foundations and parent advocacy groups are actively educating the society regarding the etiologies of disabilities, dispelling superstitious views, and promoting positive views toward individuals with disabilities.

SPECIAL EDUCATION POLICIES AND FAMILY SUPPORT IN TAIWAN

In Taiwan, children with disabilities are classified into 12 categories, which are nearly identical to the U.S. disability classification. The 2011 census in Taiwan stated that of the 3,098,631 total students, 88,002 (2.84%) receive special education services (Department of Education of Republic of China, 2012). Intellectual disability has been increasing in prevalence over the last decade (Lai, Tseng, Hou, & Guo, 2012; Lin, 2009), representing approximately 0.75% of the population receiving special education services (Chiang & Chang, 2009).

With increased education and awareness, attitudes toward individuals with disabilities are changing. The Taiwanese disability movement has developed alongside a democratic transition (Chang, 2007), and support for children with disabilities in Taiwan has changed significantly in the past 30 years, from abandonment and institutionalization to public schools providing education based upon the student's specific needs. In 1984, Taiwan advanced its legal protection for people with disabilities through the Special Education Act, which mandated early childhood special education. Despite this advancement, many young children with disabilities remained at home. Furthermore, those who attended schools received inadequate attention to social and medical concerns. Collaboration between agencies, professionals, families, and students with disabilities were loose or, more often, did not exist at all (Wang, 1993).

Adopting Western practices, the Special Education Act of 1997, and the Enforcement Rules to the Act of Special Education of 2003 were enacted to ensure that students with disabilities were integrated in inclusive classrooms (Department of Education, 1997; Ministry of Education of Republic of China, 2008). In 2009, the Special Education Act further expanded the role of parents in their child's educational decision-making process. Parents are now encouraged to collaborate with other members of the child's professional support network (including general education teachers, special education teachers, and other specialists) regarding the student's Individualized Education Program (IEP).

Provisions for family support were further recognized when the Taiwanese government passed the People with Disabilities Rights Protection Act in 2007 (Ministry of Interior of Republic of China, 2007), which mandated the municipal and county authorities to provide family care visits and service, temporary/respite and short-term care, and training for caregivers to promote a better quality of life for families of children with disabilities (Ministry of the Interior of Republic of China, 2012). Under the People with Disabilities Rights Protection Act, the Rules for Family Care Service Providers of People with Disabilities (Ministry of Interior of Republic of China, 2007) gives finer details about family care services, including regulations and limitations for service providers. For example, it mandates that temporary/respite and short-term care be provided only by licensed social workers, trained homecare specialists from the hospital, nursing organizations, mental health organizations, physical disability and mental disorder welfare organizations, or other social welfare organizations (Ministry of the Interior of Republic of China, 2012).

PROMISING PRACTICE: PARENT ADVOCACY GROUPS

Growing Awareness

To increase the awareness and access to the various family support provisions detailed above, parent groups played a key role in the development of national recognition of the rights of individuals with disabilities and their families, stemming back to the 1960s with the first parental attempts to organize for their children with intellectual disabilities (Chang, 2007). Some of these parent groups started petitions to revise special education laws, despite resistance from the larger community. Chang recalled from a personal communication with one founding parent member of a Taiwanese intellectual disability association, "I was warned of the potential consequence of losing my job. I was also told that they could make special arrangements for my child if I withdrew from the parents' organization" (Chang, 2007, p. 9). Over time, these parent organizations, taking their lead from similar disability movements in the United States and European countries, became larger and asserted more influence on special education practice and law. Recent changes in family structure (e.g., a decrease in family size as well as a change from multigenerational family to nuclear family households) have prompted families to rely more on community assistance and public-private partnerships for support for their children with disabilities. Parent advocacy groups are playing a more important role in the provision of family support for those with children with disabilities. A Taiwanese parent of a high-school student with a learning disability commented on the important role that the advocacy groups play:

> When I was a new mother, I felt hopeless and helpless all the time. When I found out about this advocacy group, I felt like I finally found a lighthouse. I realized when I receive support and suggestions from those who already experienced everything, I saved time figuring out everything by myself. I also avoided time making mistakes. You know, children cannot wait. After learning everything, I can't teach him from the very beginning because I might have already missed that critical learning period.

Parent advocacy groups have regular meetings with their members, including workshops, counseling sessions, consultation services, and self-help groups. These supports not only target their members' emotional needs, but also seek to educate parents about the nature of their child's disability and empirically based interventions. The majority of parent advocacy groups are organized by disability (e.g., ID or learning disability). Since Taipei City is the capital of Taiwan and has many resources, most headquarters of parent advocacy groups are located there.

Voices of Parent Advocacy Group Leaders

In order to examine the effectiveness of the parent advocacy groups, the second author of this chapter interviewed 10 parent advocacy group leaders in Taipei, Taiwan (Tang, 2012): three males and seven females, ages 36 to 55, who are leaders of six different disability advocacy groups (i.e., for autism, attention deficit hyperactivity disorder, hearing impairment, intellectual disability, learning disability, and vision impairment). Tang found that parent advocacy leaders reflected on the role of parent advocacy groups in providing critical emotional support and guidance that was lacking from their surrounding communities (including lack of support from fellow family members, friends, and the broader community). The parent advocacy leaders expressed that many family members, especially in-laws and fathers, are less likely to accept children's disabilities and often blame the mothers. For example, one leader of a learning disability parent advocacy group said,

> Many in-laws believe having a problematic child is a mother's fault. They think, "It is impossible to be our son's fault. We don't have any bad genes. It must be you (the mother), you pass bad genes on to the child." Sometimes, they also blame the mother for not being responsible: "You are not strict enough." "It is your fault that you don't know how to teach your kid. This is why he is always behind at school. It is not my grandson's fault."

When family members cannot accept a child's disability, their focus often shifts to the mother as the primary person responsible for the child's disability, and the mother not only loses emotional support but also carries the guilt resulting from family members' blame. Additional family support is needed to help mothers cope with the guilt and stigma. Parent advocacy group members can fill this need for emotional support. For example, one leader of a learning disability advocacy group commented,

> Some mothers call me privately because she cannot let her in-laws know. Every time she called, we always talked for at least 4 hours. Even though she did the most of the talking, I feel this is also one way to support her. Other than us, whom can she talk to?

Another leader from a hearing impairment parent advocacy group stated,

> We are like brother and sisters. We talk about our children and also our personal life. When children grow up, we are also going to get older. One day maybe our children will move out and leave us, but I know we will still support each other.

Although a few parent leaders expressed that some parents perceived that Taiwanese professionals, including medical doctors and school teachers, hold stereotypes of the child's disability, lack empathy, and/or lack knowledge about available resources, many Taiwanese parents value suggestions from professionals over laypersons. For example, as illustrated in the following comment, parents feel more confident after the professional validates and recognizes their parenting.

> You know, we are always afraid that, "Did I do this wrong?" If people around me tell me today that I did something right, I will still have doubt. But if a doctor, professional, or scholar tells me, "You are doing great. Your son can do this because of you," I then feel I am a good mother.

Several parent advocacy leaders indicated that giving positive comments to children with disabilities indirectly influences parents' view of themselves. Complaints about children's problem behaviors and poor school performance only increased parent's level of stress. One leader from a learning disability parent advocacy group shared,

> My son's teacher has never judged my son's grade.... She always tells me what my son can work on and gives suggestions. I feel that I know what I can work on. She also often tells me that my son is honest and loves to help others. At least I know she doesn't feel my son is a bad student even though he has poor school performance.

Tang (2012) found that when giving medical and professional suggestions, advocacy group leaders advise maintaining flexibility about what works for different families and being patient and open to learn from families—all of which can help develop productive relationships.

Parents Association for Persons With Intellectual Disabilities (PAPID)

Background
Because the Parents Association for Persons with Intellectual Disabilities (PAPID) is one of the largest parent advocacy groups in Taiwan, the remainder of this chapter will focus on this particular group. PAPID was officially founded in 1992 by Taiwanese parents of children with ID, however, its roots stem back to some of the first parent organizations in the 1960s (Chang, 2007). One of the primary goals of PAPID has been to promote full implementation of current laws and policies, advocate for new legislation, and expand funding for parents in the national budget. After 17 years of advocacy, PAPID now has 41 local chapters (the Taipei City chapter has

the most members: 1,322 in 2012), 14 foundations, 18 welfare centers/ institutions, and more than 15,000 active members across Taiwan (PAPID, 2008). The leaders of PAPID are ones with higher educational level and social economic status, while PAPID members represent varied ages, job fields, and educational levels. Parents of children with ID often are connected with PAPID through word-of-mouth from other families, as well as through their website and publications.

PAPID works to promote a comprehensive lifelong caring system for individuals with intellectual disabilities and their families. Primary activities include emphasizing the importance of early intervention, developing individualized education programs, advocating for legal rights of individuals with ID, promoting community-based services, conducting professional training, elevating public awareness, and furthering activities that enhance the quality of life for individuals with disabilities and their families (PAPID, 2008). Each PAPID also has trained social workers who provide additional family support services, including helping families throughout the Individualized Family Support Plan process. Parents can receive consultation services through phone, email, and/or face-to-face conversation regarding special education, early intervention, respite/short-term care, and rights and benefits for individuals with disabilities. Further, PAPID offers free training programs to individuals looking to become licensed social workers as well as free job training and opportunities for adults with intellectual disabilities.

Leaders Voices

The following section includes voices from three leaders from intellectual disability parent advocacy groups who were willing to participate in in-depth interviews subsequent to the 2012 study by Tang (2012). One PAPID leader mentioned that when Taiwanese parents first find out about their child's disability, they usually experience feelings of loss and hopelessness. Compared to recommendations from parents of children without disabilities, suggestions and encouragement from parents who have experienced raising a child with an ID were considered much more valuable. Another PAPID leader also commented that PAPID members are not just involved in PAPID activities together, but they also develop close friendships over time due to their shared parental experiences. He said,

> All my close friends are in the association and our families meet often. Honestly, raising a child with disability is difficult and after having this child, taking care of my daughter pretty much takes my whole time. My world is spinning around this child. It is the same for my wife and also many other families in PAPID. At first, we talked about children, then we take care of and support each other.

PAPID Activities

Workshops. When children first enter the school system, parents are often confused about their rights and what special education services they are entitled to. PAPID offers free workshops on current special education laws, available resources in Taiwan, and issues parents of children with ID commonly face. These workshops are usually held at public schools, especially public elementary schools, after school. Veteran parents in PAPID, who have knowledge in special education laws and policies, lead the workshops. One parent leader said,

> I have a parent who just joined our group and realized there are homecare services available for her family. Her child is already 10 years old, which is 3 years older than my child, and I have already used the service for more than five years, yet she just found out about it. If you don't look for services, services won't find you, so we always encourage parents to come to our workshops unless they know how to find resources and know the system very well.

Group discussions are included at the end of each workshop, which allow parents to share their experiences and feelings, and problem-solve together. One parent advocacy leader said, "The group discussion at the end [of each workshop] is really fun. Parents can talk to each other and maybe learn from each other. They exchange contact information." PAPID also offers free workshops for parents at their center on effective communication skills, problem-solving skills, and advocacy skills. Workshop participants not only gain professional knowledge but also have the opportunities to meet other parents who share the same experiences.

Among all the organized workshops, the PAPID leaders indicated that the workshop on the process of forming an IEP is one of the most popular ones. This workshop focuses on the general IEP processes, how to form IEP goals, and important tips for parents. The IEP workshops target parents whose children have just entered the school system and are looking for further information on special education. Two of the parent advocacy leaders mentioned that "some special education teachers may trick parents, if they know parents do not know how the IEP works." One PAPID leader provided an example: "One of our parents came to me and said she feels strange signing a blank IEP. I told her that it is wrong [to ask for a signature on a blank IEP]. She then told me she has been signing a blank IEP for 2 years." Another PAPID leader said that many special education teachers write the same goal every year because "it is easy and parents may never realize it." The IEP is intended to be an important safeguard to secure the children's rights in receiving appropriate education. There is a need for parents to be familiar with the IEP development process.

Phone and in-person support. Besides attending workshops, parents can also contact PAPID via phone for advice and support and request for face-to-face consultation. Phone calls are answered by social workers or senior PAPID members, who have rich experiences and knowledge about the special education process. One senior member commented,

> We have a lot of senior members here and they are here because they want to serve families like them. Even though I am the executive director of the group, I don't get paid. I enjoy this job, or maybe I should say it's an interest or hobby.

PAPID's helpline and one-on-one consultation services often become parents' outlets for expressing their feelings and getting feedback from people who understand their situation. One parent leader said, "They call and chat for hours because they need an ear who can listen and understand their feelings." In addition, social workers and/or senior members use these opportunities to encourage and recognize the efforts parents have made. One leader said,

> We have to admit that in Taiwanese society, people with disabilities are often stigmatized, as well as their families. Parents' hard work is easily overlooked. They really need someone to tell them, "You already do your best. You are responsible parents"—or anything like that. I wish I had this when I was raising my daughter.

Respite care. The other service that PAPID facilitates is respite care, as contracted by the government. This service is provided either in-home or in the closest PAPID center. Funding from the government is not always adequate to cover the entire expense, therefore, PAPID has several sponsors from private companies to supplement government funds. One father explained that his child can have up to 480 hours of respite care per year and after the government covers two thirds of expenses, the family pays a relatively low fee, only 45 New Taiwanese Dollars (equivalent to about U.S. $1.50) per hour. One parent advocacy leader commented on the extreme need for respite services:

> A lot of our members do not have much time for their own activities. Everything is about their child. Their child is their world. They isolate themselves from their old friends and relatives, not because they do not want to spend time together, but because they do not have time.... During weekends, parents need to bring the child to receive intervention and during weekdays people usually leave the office around 8 p.m. Some parents pick up their children from the grandparents around 9 p.m. and then return to work.

Short-term daycare and respite care are considered by participants to be the most practical and direct support for families of children with disabilities. With daycare and respite care services, parents can finally take a break from parenting and have time to invest in their personal interests and attend to other family needs. Another father expressed high satisfaction of the provided respite service:

> When I am busy and my wife needs to work overtime, I can call the association and they will arrange a staff to come over for 2 to 3 hours or sometimes it can be up to 8 hours to take care of my child. Though there is no intervention provided, the staff can bring the child to have a walk or play at a neighborhood park.

Overall, the three parent leaders of PAPID reported their members to have high satisfaction with their participation in PAPID and felt supported in a number of ways: (a) they perceived their efforts to support their children with ID were recognized; (b) they perceived their suggestions and complaints were heard by others; (c) they received suggestions and solutions from other parents; (d) they learned from members' experiences and appreciated other parents' sharing of their "mistakes;" (e) they gained more knowledge regarding special education laws and their child's disability; (f) they learned about important community resources and how to better navigate the school system; (g) they felt less isolated by participating in formal and informal activities with other parents of children with disabilities; (h) they felt that their experiences meaningfully impacted other families and that the shared experiences led to a more positive view of their own family life; and (i) overall, they felt more knowledgeable, confident, and effective as parents and citizens. A father summed up,

> I feel I am not the only one and there are many other families who experience the same. I become less worried about my child and feel I can be supported. Out of all these families, there must be one family who can help me and has the same experience.

REFLECTIONS

In a society where the cultural norm emphasizes the preservation of family and societal harmony, parents of children with disabilities in Taiwan are likely to be more vulnerable to social stigma of disability. Families tend to be more reluctant to disclose their child's disability and seek services and support. More recent social and educational reforms, however, have impacted the acceptance of disability and the provision of family support in Taiwanese society. In particular, grassroots efforts have led to the formation of parent advocacy groups to address the particular needs of families who feel stigmatized, isolated, and immobilized by traditional beliefs about disability. The present study interviewed leaders of several parent advocacy groups. Their voices indicate that the practices of the parent advocacy groups are successful in helping the parents to feel less isolated, more supported, knowledgeable and empowered, and to see positive aspects of having a child with a disability in their lives. Such findings are consistent with the research literature that suggests how important it is for parents to organize themselves and advocate for the rights of their children with disabilities and for parents to feel empowered through their participation in the process of advocacy.

As a potential model for other sites, lessons learned from this study regarding strategies, constraints, and limitations may be useful. With regard to strategies in establishing a parent advocacy group, both parents and professionals may take active roles. Parents can begin by establishing networks through various venues. For example, through schools, Taiwanese parents connect to other classroom parents by word of mouth and meet at "Parents Day" (a day for parents and teachers to meet) and field trips. Parents of children with disabilities also connect in waiting rooms of professional/hospital facilities where their children receive services or interventions from specialists, such as speech and language therapists and occupational therapists. In addition, parents network via various community venues such as local churches, temples, libraries, and activity/sports centers. Parents also use various social media networks (blogs, bulletin boards, and social networking services) to bring together other parents of children with disabilities. Through various social media networks, parents post questions, responses, and comments; they discuss specific special education-related topics and share stories/experiences online.

Professionals can facilitate the networking of parents in various ways. Due to issues of confidentiality, professionals will not share their clients' contact information; but when a parent leader wants to reach out to other parents, he/she can provide contact information, and professionals can facilitate by posting and sharing that information with other parents (e.g., via office bulletin boards or a flyer provided by the parent leader). Through educational workshops, professionals can also help parents to network with each other. These workshops encompass all topics related to special education, such as helping parents to be knowledgeable about IEP and how to help children with disabilities to maintain and generalize taught skills (e.g., money exchange at various venues such as eateries, bookstores, supermarkets, etc.). These workshops can be held by different professionals, such as speech and language therapists, special education teachers, doctors, psychologists, and social workers, as well as parents of children with disabilities. As part of the workshops and lectures, professionals can provide time for parents to interact; they can also create group activities for parents to share experiences or discuss certain topics. Having parent advocacy group leaders lead a workshop is also a way for parents to know the purposes and benefits of joining and being part of a parent group. Once a parent advocacy group is formed, professionals can post the group contact information online or at offices for other interested parents to join.

Some limitations and constraints associated with the establishment of parent advocacy groups are noted. Many parents of children with disabilities in Taiwan are reluctant to join parent advocacy groups due to social stigmatization, inability to accept their own child's disability, and lack of support from surrounding family members. In the interviews, parent advocacy leaders reflected that some parents, particularly mothers, did not feel that their family members supported their participation in parent advocacy groups. For example, one mother-in-law perceived the joining and participation in such a group to be socially frivolous. In fact, the mother-in-law claimed that her grandson's poor school performance was due to the irresponsibility of the mother because she did not spend enough time with her child. A constraint voiced by some parents is the membership cost. All parent advocacy groups in Taiwan require their members pay an annual membership fee. For example, the yearly membership fee for the Taipei PAPID branch is 200 New Taiwanese Dollars (equivalent to about U.S.$7). Even though the relatively low fee is affordable for most families in Taipei, many parents do not want to pay to join the group because direct services for their children are not provided by the organization; they do not see the need to pay solely for networking purposes. However, the majority of the interviewees of this project mentioned that they still welcomed parents to attend workshops and were willing to provide the needed support even for unofficial members. Moreover, for some small parent advocacy groups, membership may fluctuate or dwindle due to the fact that many parents will drop out after their children graduate from high school. In addition, while parent advocacy groups have been established in some rural areas and more efforts are being made in rural expansion, fewer families in rural areas are aware of the groups' existence and hence the participation in rural Taiwan is relatively low. Due to more limited social media access in rural areas of Taiwan, information flyers can be posted and made available in various rural professional/community venues. For all sites, rural and urban, quality leadership was perceived as vital to the stability of the organization.

While parent advocacy may be a means of improving services, it can also be stressful and emotionally draining for the families. Hence, the government can take a more active, rather than reactive, role to lessen the added burden on parents. Furthermore, family support policy should emphasize a family-centered service approach wherein both child and family are the focus of service programs so that parents of children with disabilities can be empowered through the service to become partners of professionals to work together for better service outcomes.

In sum, parent advocacy groups in Taiwan continue to work to educate its citizens to respect and appreciate personal differences and positively view disability. It is anticipated that further work by such groups will improve the status of individuals with disabilities in Taiwanese society and around the world.

REFERENCES

Azzopardi, A. (2000). A case study of a parents' self-advocacy group in Malta: The concepts of "inclusion, exclusion and disabling barriers" are analysed in the relationship that parents have with professionals. *Disability and Society, 15*(7), 1065–1072.

Banach, M., Iudice, J., Conway, L., & Couse, L. J. (2010). Family support and empowerment: Post autism diagnosis support group for parents. *Social Work with Groups, 33*(1), 69–83.

Berry, J. W. (1976) *Human ecology and cognitive style: Comparative studies in cultural and psychological adaptation.* New York, NY: Sage/Halsted/Wiley.

Black, A. P., & Baker, M. (2011). The impact of parent advocacy groups, the Internet, and social networking on rare diseases: The IDEA League and IDEA League United Kingdom example. *Epilepsia, 52*(s2), 102–104.

Central Intelligence Agency (CIA). (2013, April). *The CIA world factbook, East and Southeast Asia: Taiwan.* Retrieved from https://www.cia.gov/library/publications/the-world-factbook/geos/tw.html

Chang, C. (2007). Social change and the disability rights movement in Taiwan: 1981–2002. *The Review of Disability Studies: An International Journal, 3*(1), 3–19.

Chang, M. Y., & McConkey, R. (2008). Taiwanese parents who have children with an intellectual disability. *International Journal of Disability, Development and Education, 55*(1), 27–41. doi:10.1080/10349120701827961

Chiang, B., & Chang, C. F. (2009). A comparative study of special education prevalence rates by disability categories between Taiwan and Wisconsin. *International Journal of Education, 1*(1), 1–7.

Chmielowska, E., & Shih, F.-S. (2007, April). *Folk customs in modern society: "Tradition of Zuoyuezi" in Taiwan: A physical anthropology perspective.* Paper presented at the EATS IV Conference, Stockholm, Sweden. Retrieved from http://www.soas.ac.uk/taiwanstudies/eats/eats2007/file38472.pdf

Cunconan-Lahr, R., & Brotherson, M. J. (1996). Advocacy in disability policy: Parents and consumers as advocates. *Mental Retardation, 34*, 352–358.

Department of Education of the Republic of China. (1997, May). *The Special Education Act.* Retrieved from http://law.moj.gov.tw/Eng/LawClass/LawAll.aspx?PCode=H0080027

Department of Education of the Republic of China. (2012, October). Special education statistics of Taiwan in 2011. Retrieved from Special Education Transmit Net: http://www.set.edu.tw/sta2/contact/101上頁面.asp

Directorate-General of Budget, Accounting and Statistics, Executive Yuan, Republic of China. (2011, July). *Social Indicators 2011*. Retrieved from http://ebook.dgbas.gov.tw/public/Data/331311353471.pdf

Guralnick, M. J., Hammond, M. A., Neville, B., & Connor, R. T. (2008). The relationship between sources and functions of social support and dimensions of child and parent-related stress. *Journal of Intellectual Disability Research, 53*(12), 1138–1154.

Ho, H-Z., & Chen, W.-W. (2013). Taiwan. In D. Ness & C.-L. Lin (Eds.), *International education: An encyclopedia of contemporary issues and systems* (pp. 407-413). Armonk, NY: M.E. Sharpe.

Ho, H-Z., Chen, W.-W., & Kung, H.-Y. (2008). Taiwan. In I. Epstein (Gen. Ed.) & J. Pattnaik (Sec. Ed.), *The Greenwood encyclopedia of children's issues worldwide* (pp. 439–464). Westport, CT: Greenwood.

Ho, H-Z., Chen, W-W., Tran, C. N., & Ko, C.-T. (2010). Parental involvement in Taiwanese families. *Childhood Education, 86*(6), 376–381.

Ho, H-Z., Ko, C.-T., Tran, C. N., Phillips, J. M., & Chen, W.-W. (2013). Father involvement in Taiwan: A progressive perspective. In J. Pattnaik (Ed.), Father involvement in young children's lives (pp. 329–342). Long Beach, CA: Springer.

Ho, H-Z., Yeh, K.-H., Wu, C.-W., Tran, C. N., & Chen, W.-W. (2012). Father involvement in students' education in Taiwan. In H.-Z. Ho & D. B. Hiatt-Michael (Eds.), *Promising practices for fathers' involvement in children's education* (pp. 41–57). Charlotte, NC: Information Age.

Holroyd, E. E. (2003). Chinese cultural influences on parental caregiving obligations toward children with disabilities. *Qualitative Health Research, 13,* 4–19. doi:10.1177/1049732302239408

Kalyanpur, M., Harry, B., & Skrtic, T. (2000). Equity and advocacy expectations of culturally diverse families' participation in special education. *International Journal of Disability, Development and Education, 47*(2), 119–136.

Lamorey, S. (2002). The effect of culture on special education services: Evil eyes, prayer meetings, and IEPs. *Teaching Exceptional Children, 34*(5), 67–71.

Lai, D. C., Tseng, Y. C., Hou, Y. M., & Guo, H. R. (2012). Gender and geographic differences in the prevalence of intellectual disability in children: Analysis of data from the national disability registry of Taiwan. *Research in Developmental Disabilities, 33*(6), 2301–2307.

Law, M., King, S., Stewart, D., & King, G. (2001). The perceived effects of parent-led support groups for parents of children with disabilities. *Physical & Occupational Therapy in Pediatrics, 21*(2/3), 29–48.

Lin, J. D. (2009). Population with intellectual disability based on 2000–2007 national registers in Taiwan: Age and gender. *Research in Developmental Disabilities, 30*(2), 294–300.

Liu, G. Z. (2001). *Chinese culture and disability: Information for U.S. service providers.* Buffalo, NY: Center for International Rehabilitation Research Information and Exchange.

Ministry of Education of Republic of China. (2008, June). *National report on special education in Taiwan* (Publication No. 4). Retrieved from http://open.nat.gov.tw/OpenFront/gpnet_detail.jspx?gpn=2009001086

Ministry of the Interior of Republic of China. (2007, February). *People with Disabilities Rights Protection Act*. Retrieved from http://glrs.moi.gov.tw/EngLawContent.aspx?id=43

Ministry of the Interior of Republic of China (2012, July). *The rules for family care service providers of people with disabilities*. Retrieved from http://www.moi.gov.tw/dsa/news_content.aspx?sn=6506

Parents' Association for Persons with Intellectual Disability, R.O.C. (PAPID). (2008). *Parents association for persons with intellectual disabilities*. Retrieved from http://www.papmh.org.tw/ugC_English.asp

Pillsbury, B. L. (1978). "Doing the month": Confinement and convalescence of Chinese women after childbirth. *Social Science & Medicine. Part B: Medical Anthropology, 12*, 11–22.

Sadoski, C. M. (1999). *Family-school partnerships and the efficacy of parent support groups*. (Doctoral dissertation). Retrieved from http://search.proquest.com.proxy.library.ucsb.edu:2048/docview/619441371?accountid=14522. (1999-95001-211).

Sheng, V. (1999). Gender equality: Helping the disabled is helping ourselves. *Taiwan review*. Retrieved November 1, 2012, from http://taiwanreview.nat.gov.tw/ct.asp?xitem=1357&ctnode=1359&mp=1

Solomon, M., Pistrang, N., & Barker, C. (2001). The benefits of mutual support groups for parents of children with disabilities. *American Journal of Community Psychology, 29*(1), 113–132.

Tang, M. C. (2012). *Family support for families of children with disabilities in Taiwan: Voices of parent advocacy leaders* (Unpublished master's thesis). University of California, Santa Barbara.

Turnbull, A. P., & Turnbull, H. R. (1996). Participatory action research. In National Council on Disability, *Improving the implementation of the Individuals with Disabilities Education Act: Making schools work for all of America's children. Supplement* (pp. 685–711). Washington DC: National Council on Disability.

Turnbull, A. P., & Turnbull, H. R. (2001). Self-determination for individuals with significant cognitive disabilities and their families. *Journal of the Association for Persons with Severe Handicaps, 26*(1), 56–62.

Wang, M., Mannan, H., Poston, J., Turnbull, A. P., & Summers, J. A. (2004). Parents' perceptions of advocacy activities and their impact on family quality of life. *Research & Practice for Persons with Severe Disabilities, 29*(2), 144–155.

Wang, T. M. (1993). Families in Asian cultures: Taiwan as a case example. In J. L. Paul, & R. J. Simeonsson (Eds.), *Children with special needs* (pp. 165–178). Orlando, FL: Harcourt Brace Jovanovich College Publishers.

Zhou, Q. Y. (2000). *Disability welfare and social work*. Taipei, Taiwan: Wu Nan.

LIST OF CONTRIBUTORS

Terese C. Aceves	Associate Professor School of Education Loyola Marymount University
Adrienne L. Anderson	Doctoral Candidate Department of Special Education and Child Development University of North Carolina at Charlotte
Kwok Ching Chan	Student Guidance Counselor CNEC Lau Wing Sang Secondary School Hong Kong
Tak-foo Cheng	Principal CNEC Lau Wing Sang Secondary School Hong Kong
Vivian I. Correa	Professor Department of Special Education and Child Development University of North Carolina at Charlotte
Whitney J. Detar	Researcher, Koegel Autism Center Gevirtz Graduate School of Education University of California-Santa Barbara

Michael P. Evans   Assistant Professor
                      School of Education, Health & Society
                      Miami University

Ignacio Higareda   Associate Professor
                      School of Education
                      Loyola Marymount University

Hsiu-Zu Ho   Professor, Department of Education
                      Gevirtz Graduate School of Education
                      University of California-Santa Barbara

Rebekka J. Jez   Adjunct Professor
                      Department of Special Education
                      San Jose State University

Dana Kalek   Director of Operations
                      Child Development Institute-Woodland Hills, CA

Lusa Lo   Associate Professor
                      College of Special Education and Human
                      Development
                      University of Massachusetts Boston

Ya-yu Lo   Associate Professor
                      Department of Special Education and Child
                      Development
                      University of North Carolina at Charlotte

Gloria E. Miller   Professor
                      Child, Family, and School Psychology Program
                      University of Denver

Tracy Mueller   Associate Professor
                      School of Special Education
                      University of Northern Colorado

Vy Nguyen   School Psychologist
                      Cherry Creek School District, CO

Katherine Swart   Doctoral Candidate
                      Department of Special Education and Child
                      Development

Min Chia Tang   Education Specialist
                      Gevirtz Graduate School of Education
                      University of California-Santa Barbara

Mian Wang   Associate Professor
                      Gevirtz Graduate School of Education
                      University of California-Santa Barbara

CPSIA information can be obtained at www.ICGtesting.com
Printed in the USA
LVOW04s1322100415

433972LV00021B/26/P

9 781623 966317